Dear Lynne,
'For I know the plans
I have for you'...
Praying God blesses you
as He opens up those
plans.

Helen x

Choosing Extraordinary

Living out the God given dreams
you've always wanted to...

Helen Cottee

Dedicated to all those who have walked this journey with me through the ups and downs. For my husband and my babies – I love love love you, you are all I could have ever wanted; to the girls who held my hand and listened to my ramblings and ultimately gave me the kick to actually get this written - specific thanks to Clare and Penny without whom there would be no semi-colons or full stops in this book. Thank you to Kerith Community Church - you helped me to grow and find faith and become the person I am today. To the Bunters and the Cottees – the very best family a girl could have.

And finally to God – the one who enveloped and underpinned and inspired and enabled me to have a life worth living.

Contents

Prologue

It's a strange thing to write a book about choosing to live an extraordinary life. It can somehow have the power to make you feel anything but extraordinary. In fact on a very regular basis the question slithers through my mind 'Who on earth am I to be talking about this?'

But that, my friend, is entirely the point. Who am I? Who is anyone? Where does this niggle inside us to do something noteworthy come from? Are we to believe the message that it's every man for himself; that the best route for us as human beings is to progress on with our lives with no regard for anyone else? Or is there something greater planted in each one of us that pushes us on to live a life that matters; to do something that matters; to be someone that makes a difference in the world; to connect and impact and inspire?

Well, I for one think the answer is an unequivocal, resounding "yes". I think we were built to dream big dreams and to live out spectacular lives. I think we were cut from a cloth which is anything but ordinary and I am finding that the more I look, the more incredible people there are out there; some famous, others not; some noticed, others very much under the radar. People who are using who they are and what they have to do something extraordinary with their lives and, more often than not, prove to have an earth changing impact on the fortunate people who cross their path.

We have a big youth group at our church. Hundreds of teens gather every Friday night to meet and mingle and find out about faith. There is something about this group of youngsters that is inspiring. They still have that natural in-built desire to be extraordinary. They don't have dreams of normal or dull, of everyday or average. They dream big, they expect big, and they seem to have the confidence to believe it to be entirely possible.

I used to be like that. I wanted to connect; to find others who shared the searchings within me. I wanted to inspire and be inspired. I wanted my life to matter. I had dreams and I was completely sold out on seeing them happen.

I see it in many people around me, and I certainly see it in myself, that we stop dreaming the big dreams, or simply leave our dreams as just that. We don't step out to do the things we love or to pursue the desires we have. With each passing year the idea of doing something extraordinary seems less and less likely, and more and more like a fanciful daydream. There are still niggles which are stirred up when we see someone else stepping out. A tiny 'What if...' that bubbles up every now and again through the drudge of average. These bubbles float upwards like renewed hope, lifting the desire actually to do it, do the big thing, dream the big dream again... But within days, maybe even hours or minutes, the bubbles are burst with the next load of washing, or argument with our teenage son, or the repetitive siren of the alarm clock signaling another day at the office.

We let go of our dreams because of mortgages and bills to pay, responsibilities, a gradual settling down and growing up, the risk of looking foolish for even trying. Those amazing dreams and big ideas just become childish images of lives which probably would never have been anyway.

The thing is... I believe we were meant to live out those childish ideas; I think there is a deep rooted desire in every person to do something which matters and leave a mark on this earth and the people who live on it. I think we were created to be more than mediocre and greater than average. I believe we're supposed to encourage those bubbles, and grasp the hope and step into the fear of foolishness.

I believe this is because we have a piece of eternity crafted into our soul which cries out to do something which will last for ever. I have no doubt in my mind that human beings and everything we see around us was created by a being so much greater than ourselves that we can't wrap our heads around whatever that entity is.

That entity is generally known as God.

A maker, a craftsman, a creator, who shapes and moulds things of beauty, laced with his genetic mark, formed in his image. When you see some of the amazing sights in our solar system, the beautiful parts of our world, the spectacular light shows of our night skies, the incredible wonders of our oceans, they seem to point to a greater being who designed things to be extraordinary, deliberately created for purpose and worth. I find it impossible to believe that the wonders I see around me are an accident. I find it harder to believe that any one of the amazing human beings on this planet was a mistake either.

It is that ripple of the eternal which exists deep in every person that fuels the desire to live a life less ordinary. The bible, a letter from our creator to us, explains His passion for us to do just that. To step out, and step up, and live out and speak up. It calls us to a life of abundance, filled up and flowing over. It encourages that deep seed of desire to risk in order to be something wonderful.

Before I became a Christian, I thought that going to church meant giving up on interesting and exciting. I thought Christianity was about rules and commands and shouldn't do's and can't touch's. I was wrong. Since realising that I was created by a God who loves me and has plans for my life which are beyond anything I could hope for or imagine, I have started to slowly chip away at the blanket of ordinary which has shrouded and restricted my life. Learning about a God of unlimited potential and never ending boundaries has helped me to shake off some of the fear of failure in order to search for those sparkles of extraordinary which are glimmering in each of us.

This book is my journey into the discovery of extraordinary, about shrugging off the everyday in favour of something greater. It is about embracing the unknown and striding out even if fear still has an icy grip on my chest.

I hope that on the days when you feel like the only option is chocolate and pyjamas; when the lie that you are worth little (or maybe even nothing) becomes the only reality you live by - on those days, pick up this book, open it somewhere and be inspired by someone who has worked through that lie to the truth that they are worth a great deal.

The times when you feel chained by ordinary, when you wonder what on earth it's all for, or just on the regular, comfy-jeans-wearing, washing the dishes, mowing the lawn kind of day - on those days, pick up this book and allow God to speak to you about how amazing He thinks you are.

The root of this message is that I believe we were prepared before we were born to be extraordinary, I guess the question is whether *you* are prepared to believe that for your life? Are you willing to embrace your worth and discover your purpose? Are you able to journey through the things that would hold you back to live a life of value and impact?

This book is written by a Christian and God is woven through each and every page. This is the perspective I write from and whatever you believe I ask you to allow the words and the message of this book to challenge you. This is written for anyone who feels the niggle to step out. Christian or not, I think the same rules apply.

This is a book either to read cover to cover or to dip in and out of. Feel free to start in the middle if you prefer. Read it on your own or grab a group of people you trust and read it together over a cup of tea or a bottle of something tasty. Read it however you want. My prayer is simply this... that you are encouraged and inspired; that you learn from those who have gone before you; that you look at yourself differently once the words have tiptoed into your heart. I pray this prayer over each of you.

Pause and Ponder

At the end of the chapters in this book I have carved out a space, literally and metaphorically, for you to stop, take a moment, and consider if there is anything which needs a little more thought – the opportunity to pause and ponder. The thoughts in this book are based on the path that I am walking, which is a unique path designed just for me. My hope is that these pages help you to apply some of the thoughts and musings from this book to your unique path. There are questions posed which will prompt some areas of discussion or thought - use them or ignore them at will! This moment of time to pause and reflect on yourself and your path is a gift which you are free to use as you wish. Please take the gift, take the time, take the opportunity to pause before the rest of your day crowds in.

Permission

I thought I'd start by telling you a bit about me. Feel free to picture me as you like (I'm happy to run with tall and leggy with billowing hair - not true, but carry on nevertheless). As I write this I am currently 33 years old, average build with a little extra stored away in case of a famine. I have two children who have just started school and are sometimes very good and other times borderline terrors and I have been married to my very patient and boundlessly forgiving husband for nine years - we have had our ups and downs. I live in a nice house in a town like many others. There's an empty juice carton on my kitchen worktop and a gaggle of stuffed toys adorning my living room floor. I own an ironing pile the size of a small skyscraper that resides (fairly permanently) on top of the tumble drier, and my hair could do with a brush, despite the fact that I've already been out in public today.

'Fascinating!' I hear you cry...

Not really. I am, and my life is, pretty normal. We have our abnormal moments as a family - some good, others not so. But all in all, we're pretty average. I'm pretty average.

By now you may be wondering why someone who is writing about 'extraordinary' has started the first chapter of their book describing how very 'ordinary' they really are.

Living a life of purpose and influence does not require a life swap with someone more interesting than you. You don't need to hand in your notice, abandon the washing up or never do a jot of DIY again to stop being ordinary. Extraordinary is about living with the spectacular and the standard hand in hand. It is about re-coupling the sacred and the secular as they were designed to be. It is not despising the every-day in favour of the 'wow' moments. It is, however, recognising that the spectacular, the sacred, the 'wow' moment can exist in your life.

This chapter is about giving you permission to believe it for yourself.

For years I believed that I was nothing special. I have battled with self-esteem issues, bouts of depression, and feelings of worthlessness, and I believed the lie that I would amount to little. I lived under the illusion that when I did something well in one of the roles I had - Mum, wife, teacher, musician - that I added a little value to myself. But when things were not going so well, when the kids were a nightmare and I ended up ringing my other half in tears at 2.30pm demanding he leave work and come home immediately or be served with divorce papers, when I got an average report at work, when there was an issue with the band I led, suddenly my 'value' decreased and often shrank to nothing. I struggled to believe that I could add anything of worth to this world. The self-fulfilling prophecy of this meant that my life often panned out that way.

In the past few years something has started to shift. Through looking at the bible at what God has spoken over me and my life and slowly beginning to apply this, to believe this for myself, the lies I had built my self-esteem and worth on started to crumble. This has not been an easy or quick journey. It's often two steps forward, three steps back.

You see, I now know it to be true that I am not defined by what I do, but walking that out in my day to day life is much harder than saying it out loud. It's harder when you feel a bit disappointed. It's harder when someone is more talented than you at the thing you do. It's harder when no one seems to notice you or miss you. It's hard when other people get opportunities and you don't. It's hard when you hear 'no's' from people you love. It's basically just hard a lot of the time. I know many people feel this way. Sidelined and a bit unnoticed. Kind of useless and sort of unimportant. And so I, with many others, am continuing to learn the lesson of how to BE rather than how to DO. I am re-learning over and over that I have value that has nothing to do with the area I work in or serve in. I am slowly and painfully learning that my intrinsic value is in my eternal DNA, not in my transient day to day.

My story is one of starting to see the unfolding of a plan crafted by God. I am starting to believe that He would have a plan for me - and that it would be one which is good - for me and for others. My story is of an average person living an average life with an average amount of clutter in my house, discovering that I have been granted permission by a heavenly authority to do something of eternal worth. Why? Because worth was placed on my head when God came to earth as a man and said that my life was worth His.

He has given me permission to step out and believe it for myself. Today, if you would let me I want to hand that permission to you. Trust me, if I can believe that I am created for something of worth, you can too. There is nothing in my past that would set me apart, nothing in my educational background; if you were to walk into my house today you would see nothing that would mark me for greatness. This belief that I can be someone and do something significant is not an external thing, it is planted deep in my soul.

It would take a whole other book to pick at the thread of why it is we often feel the need for permission. Forgive the sweeping generalisation, but I think women are the worst for needing other people to justify their actions and decisions. As a woman I often need to run every decision past a group of others, I need their approval and their support. A group of nodding heads is the thing I crave to give me the confidence to take the step which I deep down know is the right one. Permission is a strange thing, of course as adults we don't actually need it but I know as a human I feel a desperate desire for it.

I know in my role as a Mum I have often felt the need for permission, possibly more strongly than in any other area of my life. When someone else says they give their kids chips for dinner, it gives me permission to stop pretending I always craft beautifully organic dinners. Sometimes, we too eat chips and ketchup for dinner. When someone else says their house looks like bomb site most of the time, it releases something in me that I don't have to be super woman all the time. When another bedraggled individual owns up that at times they find parenting hard and that they get it wrong on a regular basis, I feel the weight of trying to get it right all the time lift - I too am allowed to be a bit bedraggled and not perfect. It's okay, I'm not alone.

I think the same applies to the positive things in our world. When someone else says they're happy with the way they look and it's not like the women in magazines, it gives me permission to be a bit happier with myself. When someone else declares that they are proud of something they have achieved, I feel I can be too. When someone else who is a bit like me chooses to do something inspiring, I feel permission to choose to do something inspiring of my own.

The guest speaker at one of our women's conferences at church was Shauna Niequist. She is a member of a church called Willow Creek Community Church in Chicago and she is a writer. She was asked in an interview 'Did you always want to be a writer?'. Her answer... 'Yes, but like you want to be an astronaut when you're a kid'.

The thing is, she was actually doing it. This mum of two with a husband and a house to look after was doing the thing she dreamed of as a kid. She had dared to believe it possible and had worked hard actually to live out that dream.

In that moment, maybe one she won't even remember, I was granted permission to believe that my dream could be more than just a childish notion. If she could do it than why not me? If I can do it, then why not you?

The reality is that doing something extraordinary is not as glamorous as it appears. It is committing to something day after day, it is about hard work and dedication. It takes knowing yourself and being willing to use all the bits of yourself to do something you passionately believe in. It means still cooking the dinner and chipping away at the ironing ~~skyscraper~~ pile and fixing the leak under the toilet and holding down the day job... whilst you write that book, or take that course, or help that family, or volunteer for a charity or whatever else is in your heart. It is then stepping back and allowing God to take it and use it wherever and however He wills. 'Not my will but yours.'

My favourite passage in the bible is found in Jeremiah 29:11:

"For I know the plans I have for you," declares the Lord, "plans to prosper you and not to harm you, plans to give you hope and a future."'

God has a plan for each of us. He speaks hope over our lives, and he has been gently whispering that plan to us. He calls you to hear His voice and believe it for yourself, to do the hard work and step out even when it's scary and dare to live it. He asks that we would do all we can do coupled with Him doing what only He can do.

God believes in you. Maybe it's time for you to believe in yourself. If you are like me and feel the need for permission to step out or to allow your mind to gently lean towards the notion that you may have something great in you which is screaming to get out, with my hands clasped together in prayer for you, I hand you the permission that was so graciously handed to me.

Pause and Ponder: Permission

'For years I believed that I was nothing special.'

What thoughts and emotions does this statement summon up in you?

'She had dared to believe it possible.'

Are there things you dreamed of doing or being that you have stopped daring to believe possible?

'God believes in you. Maybe it's time for you to believe in yourself.'

If someone could grant you permission to do anything, what would you do?

No ordinary child

This is where our story begins; the story of being extraordinary and it is one of my favourite stories. I love it because it narrates the tale of a regular man whose life was pretty chaotic, who had a passion which burned in his belly, had the opportunity to stand up and be counted and did so despite many obstacles. If this story doesn't inspire the opportunity to be extraordinary, I'm not sure anything else will.

This is the story of Moses.

If you don't know the story, I'll give you the abridged version...

Moses was born and should have been killed but his mother gave him up in order to protect him. He was raised as an Egyptian (the people with eye liner) rather than an Israelite (God's people; less eye liner) but Moses knew that the slavery his people lived under was wrong. When he was about forty he saw an Israelite being beaten by an Egyptian. Something burned inside him and he killed the Egyptian. This was not popular and Moses was on the most-wanted list so he fled to a place called Midian where he settled down, got a wife and kids and worked his day job as a shepherd. This all panned out well for another forty-odd years until one day whilst looking after his sheep he saw a bush on fire. Not such a life-changing event until he realised that the bush didn't burn up and it was in fact God trying to get in contact. It was here that God and Moses had a talk which was documented in the bible in the book of Exodus, chapter 3. You can find the non-abridged version there.

The conversation between God and Moses gives us a glimmer into God's desire for us in general. It shows his heart towards his people, it spells out his passion for us to stand up and be counted. Not only that, but we also get to see how a regular guy responds to such a request. If I'm honest, this is why I love this story so much. Spoiler alert - Moses tells God to find someone else - I love the honesty!

Seeds before fruit

Let's look back at Moses in Egypt at about aged forty. In Exodus 2:11-12 we read this:

> 'One day, after Moses had grown up, he went out
> to where his own people were and watched them
> at their hard labour. He saw an Egyptian beating
> a Hebrew, one of his own people.

Looking this way and that and seeing no one, he
killed the Egyptian and hid him in the sand.'

And then a few verses later we read this about Moses once he has fled to Midian:

'Now a priest of Midian had seven daughters,
and they came to draw water and fill the troughs
to water their father's flock. Some shepherds
came along and drove them away, but Moses got
up and came to their rescue and watered their
flock.' Exodus 2:16-17.

Many years before Moses' burning bush moment, decades before God called him to stand up for the justice of the Israelites, we see the seeds of justice planted in Moses' heart. I don't believe that God just happened upon Moses one day and thought 'Oh, I suppose that shepherd will do as the one to save my people'. I think God knew that there was something which was part of Moses' DNA which wanted to fight against injustice in his world. He had risked his life in Egypt once before, God saw that spark, God had planted that seed, he knew that fighting against injustice was what Moses was passionate about.

Seeds don't grow into beautiful fruit trees overnight and fruit does not appear as soon as you plant a seed. There is an extended time of watering and feeding and weeding out rubbish which is needed for the seed to grow enough that it becomes a plant which can sustain fruit. There are seeds in each of us. Desires, tendencies, passions, ideas, abilities... little seeds which we may not even know are there but which, with the right attention, can one day become mighty trees filled with much fruit.

I used to think God's blessings on us were kind of random, that He was standing throwing handfuls of blessings out like candy at Christmas. The older I get, the more I think God chooses our blessings carefully and specifically, just as He does our talents and temperaments. It's like He created individual recipes for each of us of what we need and what will suit us best for the road set out before us. The story of Moses seems to illustrate this. These seeds planted in him were what fuelled him for his task later in life, but they had been planted and were growing in him for a long time before God called him to save His people.

There will be things in each of us which we may be using or may be sat dormant. There will be things we look back at and realise were guiding us in ways we never expected. We can see little seeds and shoots growing all the time, specific seeds planted by a gardener who knows which plants are needed in each garden. What is planted in yours? What talents do you have, what desires and dreams do you hold, what things cause a burning desire in you to see change, are there things in this world you simply can't bear to leave unattended? These are the seeds God had planted in you ready for the unfolding journey you are walking with Him.

Your burning bush moment

Moses was pottering round doing his day to day job, keeping food on the table and a tent over his family's head when God stooped down and stepped into his world. God's timing is always perfect; it's not always easy to understand from a human perspective, but it is perfect none the less. God knew which year, which day, which bush He was going to use to get Moses' attention and call him up.

Have you ever had a burning bush moment? A moment in the middle of an ordinary day, an ordinary year, when God chooses to make His presence felt in a miraculous way, and calls you out? I have. It was the moment when God lit up the floor in front of me and told me I was standing on holy ground, right where I was. Just as with Moses, the normal everyday spot I was standing on, was declared holy by God Himself. Where you are, right now, is a piece of holy ground, a spot where God can meet with you. Where you are right now is where you can start to make a difference in the world.

My moment happened late one night when I was battling with my future. I had choices to make and options to consider and I prayed the simple prayer 'God what are you saying to me?'. In that moment, I felt that He told me to take off my spiritual sandals and bow before Him, as He gently called me to what He had prepared for me to do. He didn't light up a bush, He probably knew it would be a safety hazard in my bedroom, but the impact was the same for me in that moment as it was for Moses. That one burning bush moment where God stepped down changed the trajectory I was on for my future.

If you have never had a moment like this, why not ask God to speak to you clearly about your future. I can't guarantee He will in the way He did with me, but I believe God wants the best for you. He says we should ask and knock and seek. Why not carve out some time to do just that.

I think for many people, these burning bush moments are vital when we start on a new path because it marks the place where something changed. It acts as a monument to remind us of what God has said and done. Moses went on to face some incredibly tough stuff in the following months after this event, culminating in the death of his nephew and total separation from Pharaoh, the brother he had been raised with. I bet there were times in the darkest moments when he doubted what he was doing. What do you do in these moments when it's hard and you're just not sure? You look back to those monuments that remind you of what set you off on this course.

Monuments are vital for reminding us of what has been, in order to help us to keep learning the lessons and keep on going. Burning bush moments are monuments to God's call on our life.

I think back to that night in my bedroom when God connected with me and whispered purpose into my life, and when things are hard it spurs me on to keep going. I remember the promise God spoke over me and the task He called me to.

What is that in your hand?

When God met with Moses at the burning bush, Moses was a little taken aback (understandably, I hasten to add). He doubted that he was the right man for the job, he looked at his weaknesses and let them overshadow his strengths. Like many of us, he felt ill-equipped to do what God called him to. God had given him the tools he needed but in that moment, Moses wobbled. He starts asking 'what ifs'. Wow, how familiar does that sound?! What if it fails, what if no-one else believes this, what if, what if... Faith is tricky if you don't know the outcome, but that's exactly what faith is! If we had everything guaranteed before we even started, it would take no faith at all. God is in the business of growing our faith, in Him and in His promises. He calls us to be people of faith rather than people who are afraid to step out because of the 'what if's'. In response to Moses' doubts, God asks him one simple question - what is that in your hand?

Why did God choose this question to sharpen Moses' faith?

The beauty of God's calls on our life if that He only requires two things from us - the faith to step out and what is already in our hand.

What did Moses take when he went before Pharaoh? His shepherd's staff. What did God use to perform all the mighty miracles? His shepherd's staff. What parted the waters of the sea and saved a nation? His shepherd's staff. God used who Moses already was, He called him to use what was already in his hand. Moses already had the tools he needed, God was simply asking him to use them in a new way.

What is that in your hand? What do you already do, what do you already have? God is calling us to use what is already in our hand to make a difference in His world.

I am terrible at science and pretty useless at maths, but I can do words (mainly because I have so very many of them bubbling up at any given moment). It would be illogical for God to call me to impact the world as a scientist or mathematician, when He could use what is already there - my words. God doesn't need to re-create you for you to be extraordinary for Him, He needs you and what you already have in your hand. Look carefully at what you already have. How could you be using these things to make a difference for Him?

I encourage you to read the account of Moses and let it inspire you. His life is extraordinary. He was born and should have been killed; he was saved and adopted by foreigners who raised him as one of their own. He stood up for what he believed in and had to flee from all he knew because of that. He had a wait of forty years before his ministry began. God chose to meet with him and call this ordinary shepherd to greatness and then his life went on to impact an entire nation and many generations since through his bravery and faith. What a life.

You may think you are just one ordinary person whose life could have little impact. Don't believe it. You are one person who, with God on your side, could change the world around you, who could maybe even change a nation for generations to come. What is God calling you to? What is in your hand that He wants you to use? Where do you need to raise your faith level to believe you can be part of the change?

The bible tells us that Moses was no ordinary child, I am here to pass on the message - neither are you.

Pause and Ponder: No ordinary child

'What is planted in your garden?'

Are there desires, ideas, gifts, abilities in your life which maybe haven't come to fruition yet? Which seeds can you see starting to sprout?

'Have you ever had a burning bush moment?'

If you have, spend a moment reminding yourself of the details of what you felt you were called to. If not, why not take a moment to ask God to speak to you?

'What is that in your hand?'

What are you currently holding which God could use on your journey into choosing an extraordinary life?

It started with a kiss

I remember when I was a young teenager being fascinated with first dates. I was, and probably still am, a hopeless romantic. I love stories of backwards glances and just-caught smiles; of chance meetings and newly flickering friendships. I remember asking people about how they met their partner and what their first date looked like... and I'm a sucker for a chick flick. I love the classics like 'When Harry met Sally' and 'Pretty Woman'. I love the more contemporary 'Love Actually' and 'Jane Austin Book Club' types. I even love the two-star, not-really-much-of-a-storyline ones that no-one else has seen. I've probably watched them all. The thing which grabs me most about love stories is the beginnings. I do love to know how it all works out in the end but the cynic in me tends to think that a few months after the credits have finished rolling, the main characters are probably bickering about dirty dishes like the rest of us. I don't think these stories do or should end so neatly but I do love the way they start.

The thing about the start of love stories is that you often don't know they have started until you're some way into them. You don't know at the time that the brief conversation or the impromptu coincidence, the friend of a friend, the new guy in the office - will in fact turn out to be the love of your life. In the films, we're given backstage access to the story unfolding. We get to peer into the plot with a quiet narrative of what will happen in the coming scenes. In real life, of course, the unfolding of the plot is never quite so simple or predictable.

When my husband Dave and I first met, I had no idea I was going to marry him. He happened to be dating my now best mate at the time. Not the most obvious start to a love story. We were friends for a long time, we were in our church band together and had similar interests and we always shared a slightly wicked sense of humour and laughed together lots. I think other people saw little golden threads of a future developing before we did. Then one day I suddenly realised how much I looked forward to seeing him, how he made my world a bit brighter, how he made me a bit better. I hasten to add that he and my friend had gone their separate ways by this point!

After some months of shall we/shan't we, on Christmas Eve 2001 we shared our first kiss as a couple. We didn't know where it was leading, we had no details of what our future would look like, but that kiss was the first whisper of a new direction, a new trajectory of a life together.

With so many new paths, it starts with a kiss. Not a physical one, but a spiritual one. A moment where God bends down from the heavens and places his face close enough to ours for him to plant a tiny kiss of promise on our cheek. A kiss - a mark of love and affection and tenderness and care; a symbol of commitment and relationship; a sign of love; a kiss that sets us apart and speaks of a future of togetherness rather than separation.

God is a God of power and might and eternity. He holds planets and stars and solar systems in the palm of His hand. He crafts and creates and sees the beginning and the end all out of the corner of His magnificent eye and yet He chooses to reach down to brush our cheeks with tender promises. The day I realised that God was not a stern head teacher waiting to punish my mistakes but rather a relational Father who wanted my heart more than my perfection changed my life, and when it comes to being the extraordinary person God has created you to be, it is vital to be enveloped by the truth of this loving God.

I know many Christians have experienced these precious godly moments. I know many Christians who also ask the question 'was that really God?'. It can be hard to ask yourself the question of whether God was really close enough for you to feel His breath on your face. It can be hard to distinguish whether that idea really was heaven sent or your own mind meandering around inside your skull. It can be even harder to know how to act on that moment.

I'm beginning to realise that knowing and sensing the gentle touches of God on our lives is vital to us leading the extraordinary lives which we each have the capacity to lead. In a 21st century world which is permanently connected, always on, never quiet, these precious moments can be so easily drowned out. We need to learn to take the time to stop. We need to ask God to speak and expect Him to. Slowly we will learn to distinguish the whispers, to know His voice, to feel the holy kisses of promise.

Seek out the kisses

That first kiss with my husband was vital for my future. It signaled that something was different, it marked that something had changed. My life would be much less lovely had that connection not been sealed with a kiss. I would not be who I am today if it hadn't happened.

God is slowly teaching me the same lesson about spiritual kisses. These tiny marks of God's love which are gifted to us also create something more lovely, more alive, more fulfilling. We need to seek out the kisses. We may not know exactly what lies ahead on our path but the connections with God leave a little trail which one day we will look back at and say "Well I never saw that coming!". Just like a good love story, it will only be with hindsight that the conversation or decision or chance meeting will be seen to be a part of something greater. We will be able to look back and see the golden threads weaving an ornate tapestry showing the tale of a life lived well.

As we approach our 10 year anniversary, I look back at my marriage and can hardly believe what has happened. So much good that I would have never anticipated, some heartbreak that I never knew was ahead, the ups and downs and plateaus and valleys that have created a story of nuance and beauty. It's not all been easy, in fact much of it has taken hard work and commitment and lots of grace and more forgiving that I thought possible, but this is our love story. And it started with a kiss.

Our story is still being written, as is my story with God. This life I have been blessed with is still under construction but already I am starting to look back and see the amazing twists and turns I would never have anticipated. Again, the good, the bad and the ugly have been used to craft something that is starting to catch the light and tell a tale. The extraordinary is being honed in my screenplay in ways I could never have imagined.

I don't know what lies ahead or how the story will end when the credits roll. I don't know all of the characters and I certainly am oblivious to much of the plot, but I do have a God who knows it all and who whispers to me all I need if only I choose to take the time and create the space to listen.

I thank God that He is not distant and uninterested, I am grateful that He is a God of tenderness and compassion. I love that He chooses to come close enough for me to know His presence and I love that He marks my life with gentle touches which show me I am loved and valued and full of purpose in His eyes.

Pause and Ponder: It started with a kiss

'He chooses to reach down to brush our cheeks with tender promises'.

What promises has God spoken over your life?

'Well I never saw that coming!'

Sometimes it is good for our faith to look back at our lives and see the story which has unfolded – the things you expected and the things you didn't. How can you see God at work in your story so far?

Tractor ruts

It's a lesson I keep on having to learn that I am not what I do.

I like to be successful at things, I guess we all do, but as I've mentioned before, success in a job does not define who I am, although there is a tractor rut which I keep on slipping into which tells me otherwise. I slip when things are going well and I slip when they're not. I will suddenly catch myself beginning to define myself by my job, role or achievements. DANGER!

I mention this lesson throughout this book, mainly because I keep having to re-learn it and remember it, but I wanted to pause a moment to write specifically about it. This is the chapter I am going to read over and over to myself on a daily basis until the tractor ruts get less deep and my shabby old vehicle slips off the road into those ruts less and less frequently.

The problem with living a life where you valued by who you are and not what you do, is that you have to know who you are to be able to do that. It may sound obvious but I find it harder than it sounds to live out. You see we are people who like fairness. Just come round to our house when we're handing out sweets to the kiddies to witness that at its most basic. Peer in when one of my kids is reporting back on the poor behaviour of the other, screaming out (often literally) for a fair punishment to be handed out. We like justice; we like to be treated fairly. And so we struggle with grace.

The problem with grace is the 'undeserved' aspect. Undeserved does not sit well with us as a general rule. My six year old would not like it if my four year old was given a treat she didn't deserve; we struggle when people are given opportunities we feel they don't deserve; we can't cope when people don't get what they deserve for good or ill. The undeserved nature of grace is tricky for us to get our heads around.

This is why we like to define ourselves by what we do - I am a success if I achieve. There's an element where that is of course true. Doing well at your job, whether paid or unpaid, is rewarding and fulfilling and brings you success, but success does not measure your worth as a person. God measures worth very differently.

Much of the material in this book encourages you to dream your dreams again; to step out and make a difference and impact and influence; it encourages you to find out what you are good at and what God has gifted you to do; it hopes that you will choose to make a difference in the world.

This chapter pleads with you to know your value before you do any of these things.

The tractor rut that you are what you do comes from a place of not knowing your worth. It is created when human beings try to gain worth from what they can offer rather than gaining worth by who they are. Somehow the equation is backwards and confused. We have lost the truth about our value and so we try to find it from places that will be a poor substitute that will never satisfy that desire to matter.

You see, you do matter. Some of you really need to hear that. You matter a great deal. You are worth a great deal. If you have read that sentence and can't quite accept that about yourself, please go back and read it again until you do. The danger otherwise is that your quest for meaning, your desire to be extraordinary will be in order to find value, and that is not the point. You see, the reason we can live lives that are abundant and fulfilling and impacting is born from an understanding that we are creatures of worth. Doing extraordinary things does not give you worth, being crafted in the image of the creator of the universe is what makes you extraordinary. Our worth is woven into every fibre of our being by our maker; He is the One who determines our worth. We were auctioned off for a higher price than we can humanly measure in order that we could have the opportunity to use the amazing things given to us for God's glory.

Nothing you can do can balance the scales of the price paid for you. The best thing you can ever do for yourself is accept that to be the truth over your life. It stops us from trying to buy ourselves back, to try and prove that we are worth something to the One who already knows we are, because He paid the cost. He doesn't want you to have an extraordinary life in order to show you are valuable, He is the One who gave you your value before you even knew who He was, before you had achieved a single thing.

The scales will never balance on this one; your deeds will never be equal to your worth. You matter whether you feel that you deserve to or not, that's the beauty of grace; God's everything was given to you at Christ's expense not yours.

The tractor ruts which I fall into so very regularly are created by a vehicle which is fuelled by doubt and fear and a poor understanding of my inheritance as God's child. God is offering me the gift of fresh knowledge and fresh thinking, He wants me to start again from a place of security in Him and who He says I am in Him.

He is slowly getting rid of the ruts through His healing love and gentle re-crafting of my mind and heart. He whispers that I am His over and over until I get it, He is constantly showering me with His love because He is love. He starts to fix the ground and strengthen my foundations in order that He can build and that I can be involved in the building project, not so that I can matter, but because I already do.

> *'Amazing grace, how sweet the sound*
> *That saved a wretch like me*
> *I once was lost but now I'm found*
> *Was blind but now I see '[1]*

My eyes are slowly being opened to this amazing grace that saves me and sustains me and gives me hope and a future. Grace from a God who created me to matter, despite what the world would say, what my past would throw at me or what my present would suggest. He says I matter because I am His. On this basis, I stride out to leave a mark on the earth, to have impact and to live out my dreams. I slowly start to believe that this is possible for me, not out of an arrogance based on my abilities, but from a surety that I have eternal significance running through my veins.

---

[1] John Newton, 1779 Copyright Public Domain

Pause and Ponder: Tractor ruts

Are there any tractor ruts you seem to keep slipping into?   .

'I am not what I do'.

How does this apply to you?

'Nothing you can do can balance the scales of the price paid for you'.

Which things do you tend to get your worth from? Do you allow these things to determine your value? How can you start to recognise that God's scales work differently from ours?

'God created me to matter, despite what the world would say, what my past would throw at me or what my present would suggest.'

Are there things from your past, present or from the world we live in that steal your feelings of worth?

Being a princess

When I first arrived at our church, 20 years old, battered and bruised and a bit of a wreck, I joined a home group full of mums. It was not deliberate; I just ended up there by chance. Looking back it was the balm that I needed in order to learn who I was in a safe environment full of people who God had filled with tenderness and care which they not only poured onto their own kids, but also lavished onto me.

There was Nicky, the group leader, whose sofa I slept on for more nights than I can remember. She opened her heart and her home. She fed me and held me and was there when I needed a good old cry, and was the Mum I needed when mine was hundreds of miles away. I grew up in her house and found my feet under her care. She was at my graduation, my wedding and is still one of my greatest encouragers. Then there was Ali. She officially took me in when the sofa at Nicky's needed a break. I lodged with her and her family for a year. They put up with my late nights and insane messiness (they didn't see the floor of that room the whole year I lived there). She encouraged me to sing and play the piano and face many of my fears of inadequacy associated with being in the 'public eye' as part of a band. I taught her children to eat cold pizza for breakfast; she taught me how to make a mean sausage casserole and how to ice a Christmas cake, how to sing the third of a chord and how to keep going when things around you are hard and painful. Then there was Di who took me on the school run and let me help cook the dinner; I baby-sat her kids and would then sit for hours when she and her husband got home, debating points of faith. They drove me around and helped me out and gave me more than I deserved; they accepted me for who I was. I also met Karina. She was the fire cracker. Small and super-feisty and full of passion and energy. She gave me kicks up the rear end when I needed it and gentle hugs when I needed them too. I remember days in her living room playing with her kids (who called me Heaven because they couldn't say Helen), learning about what the bible said over my life.

I thank God for these women, these spiritual 'mums' who were open and kind to me, who nourished me in my early days. Throughout my journey I have been blessed with other women who have guided and mentored me. They have chosen to share their wisdom and to give away the gift of their experiences, their lessons learned, the good and the bad. It opened my eyes to the way church should work - one hand reaching forward to those ahead and one hand reaching back to those coming up behind you - a daisy chain of saints leading the way home. I encourage you to open your doors and your hearts to young people who need to be nurtured, reach back to them and hold onto them. They need you to show them that they are loved. They need to see those who are a step ahead doing life well - they will learn from you and take in more wisdom than you know. They will eat your food and maybe sleep on your sofa, they will probably mess up your house and I can guarantee they won't be perfect. For me, mums in particular were a blessing in my early 20's. To see them doing life and laundry, to watch and learn and be invited into the fold was incredibly powerful. Now, I am never happier than when I have a gaggle of youngsters gathered round my table, eating inordinate amounts of food (generally the boys, I hasten to add), laughing, learning, being part of our family. It blesses me, it blesses our children, and I pray it blesses them.

Anyway, back to one those spiritual mums... One day I was at Karina's house and she spoke a picture over my life - that was the kind of a normal, everyday occurrence when you were at Karina's. This picture has guided and encouraged and pushed me so many times in so many different situations since that day almost thirteen years ago. The picture was of a princess. Now, any of you who know me will know I'm not the 'princessy' type. My daughter is obsessively so - she is all tiaras and twirly dresses and sparkly accessories but I am not. I may have been when I was four but I grew up with three brothers so I was sooner found in a football kit than a dress, my dreams were of winning goals rather than handsome princes. I despised the view of princesses that needed a man to rescue them; I would rather rescue myself thank you very much. Anyway, Karina tended to know what she was talking about so I let the vague disdain for the princess analogy go.

She talked about how princesses are who they are because of who their father is. A girl cannot make herself a princess; she has to be the daughter of a King. A princess has the run of the Kingdom, she is not restricted in where she can go. A princess has the King's resources at her fingertips. A princess can make more of the gifts and talents that she has than a regular Joe because of her Father's influence and her inheritance. Her status is confirmed in the lineage she belongs to. Princesses are not singing, dancing Disney™ creations who need a knight on horseback to rescue them, they are part of a great family full of opportunity and promise. With the King on your side you can be destined for great things.

Now this is the sort of princess picture I could buy into.

When we accept the gift Jesus gave to us by paying the price for our spiritual darkness in order that we can be spiritually alive, we are adopted into His family. We become royalty. His Father is now our Father. The King is now known as 'Dad'. Our parentage changes and our inheritance is now the same as Jesus'. The resources which are now offered us from the King are far beyond anything we could have come by ourselves and He can grant us opportunities as a princess that would never have been available as a pauper.

I remember being pretty wow-ed by this idea as Karina spoke it out, painting a picture of a future that I never thought possible. This was what was now available to me.

Male or female, prince or princess, if you are a son or daughter of the King then this promise is true for you. God wants us to know what is there for us, what He has made available to us though our adoption into His family. But sadly, we have the title of prince or princess but often continue to live like the pauper. We don't use what is now available to us, we don't step into our new identity. We wear rags from the past whilst riches lie available and un-used. For a princess there is nothing too expensive, nothing too outlandish, no gown too grand, no jewels too valuable.

When you were adopted into God's family he made it possible for you to have your rags, your filthy garments, removed. He took any shame from anything you have ever done, He took your guilt and your pain. Instead He dressed you in a fine gown of promise, adorned you with clothes which He paid the price for that you never could have. He clothed you in righteousness and goodness and mercy. Because a crown of thorns was placed on His Son's head, He could place a crown of beauty and joy on yours. Everything He has is now your inheritance and He allows you to dip into that inheritance whenever you want. A vault overflowing with love and grace and peace.

Don't live under your past identity, choose to accept that you are now a son or daughter of the King. Live it, step into it, embrace it, choose to believe it. What resource do you need? Ask for it. The King owns the kingdom, if He knows it will bless you then He is certainly able to give it to you. Why do you expect a stone instead of bread when you ask? Don't be too afraid to ask. He's not a tyrannical King, He's a gracious one. Slow to anger and rich in love. He doesn't rule with a rod of iron but with hands of grace.

If we carry the analogy on we realise that 'extraordinary' is entirely possible for a member of the royal family. When you're just another street urchin the idea that you can do something big, something amazing, is a reach. I guess it's possible but it's certainly not going to be easy. You don't expect a princess to be ordinary though do you? You expect her to make a difference and that if she does something it can become something great. This is the basis every Christian comes from, the place of being a child of the King, a child whom the King loves so much that He would give anything He can, a child who has been handed the promise that the King will give him or her the desires of their heart as that heart is positioned to delight in the King Himself. If we love Him and we love what He loves, He will then vouch for what we do.

Delight yourself in Him. Learn about Him. Get to know Him. Find out what He is passionate about. If you give yourself over to His work, He is more than capable of enabling you to achieve something great for His glory and the sake of His Kingdom.

I am slowly learning that the very best way is to fix your heart on the right things, take what you have in your hand, give it everything you have in your will, and then hand it to the King who can do with it more than you could ever hope for or imagine. That is the best sort of princess you can be.

Pause and Ponder: Being a princess

'The King is now known as Dad'.

Does your relationship with God resemble a Father-child relationship? Christian or not, what does this relationship of God as Father mean to you?

'We wear rags from the past whilst riches lie available and unused'.

Which rags do you still cling onto? Are there things that you 'wear' that don't fit with being a son or daughter of the King? What riches lie unused in your life?

'If we carry the analogy on we realise that 'extraordinary' is entirely possible for a member of the royal family.'

Do you have faith that God can use you to do amazing things if you are a part of His family?

I want to be an octopus

One of the things I wasn't expecting when I had children was that people ask you the same questions over and over. It's like they just can't help it. When you have a baby it is 'are you breast feeding?' and 'does he sleep through yet?'. A little while later it's 'how many teeth does he have?' then 'how many words does he have?'. When the kids get a bit older, the questions are asked *to* them rather than *of* them. I remember my son once declaring very loudly that he was tired of having to tell everyone how school was. And that maybe they should listen so they didn't have to keep asking. Sweet. I guess there are only so many questions you can ask about a toddler but discussing my son's inability to sleep for over 5 years was at some points a little tiresome.

One of the questions I find myself asking my children on a regular basis, and other people often chip in with is 'what do you want to be when you grow up?'. We are fascinated with children's responses to this question. We love the humour of the child who wants to be an inanimate object like a cheese sandwich or a bucket, we 'ahhhhh' over the ones who utter something cute like a desire to be ballerina or a puppy and we have silent pride for those special few who declare from a young age that they want to be a doctor or the prime minister.

When my son William was two years old I went to Zambia. As a church we had started to partner with Tearfund and a group of churches called the Evangelical Fellowship of Zambia to help a rural community in the north of the country turn around. As with so many African nations, Zambia had been hit by HIV/AIDS in a devastating way. That, coupled with poverty, had ravaged the area we were partnering with called Serenje. I spent two and a half weeks in Zambia and it changed my life more profoundly than anything else I've ever experienced. To know that a twelve hour flight away there are people who have few clothes, little food, and no basic medication – it's gut wrenching. I held a child the same age as my son who was dying of malaria, a disease which would have cost a few pounds to either prevent or cure. I could barely hand this child back to his ten year old brother who cared for him. My view of the world and my place in it was turned on its head during that fortnight and so when I got home, the trip had a massive impact on my family too. Megan was only fourteen months old and although she likes to look at photos of 'Mummy in Africa', she doesn't really remember me going, but William certainly does. He would sit in the weeks after I got back with my photos of children, like him, and yet so very different from him. I explained to him how many of them had very little food, no toys, maybe only one set of clothes. We delicately told him how many of these children had to live with their Grandma because their Mummies and Daddies had been poorly and had died. I remember his angst about their plight and I remember his childlike declaration that we simply had to help. He would save food on his plate at dinner time to send to these kids, and he would literally be brought to tears by aid appeals for Africa on the TV. His heart was grasped by the plight of children in poverty. I believe this is a God planted seed that we shall see more of in the future.

About two years later we went through a season where we would be driving along in the car and from time to time William would come out with a random profound statement as only a four year old can. In the middle of one of our bizarre conversations I asked the much repeated question "Honey, what do you want to be when you grow up?'. His response caught me off guard slightly. 'Mummy, when I grow up, I want to be an octopus'.

Up until this point, William's response to the 'when you grow up…' question had always been one of those things you anecdote to people to get an 'ahhh' in exchange for a large amount of parental smugness. You see Will had always stated his desire to do social justice, to make a difference in the life of the world's poor. Firstly he had planned to adopt children from Zambia who didn't have enough food; then he was going to be a midwife to help babies in under-resourced countries. It was the sort of career choice any mother of a four year old would be proud of… and at the time we were in the sort of toddler stage that we really had to search for things to show off besides endless tantrums and sullen faces. The one thing I had clung to during hour long battles over the naughty stair was the fact that my son was going to grow up to be a person of social worth. And now he decided he was going to be a sea creature. Splendid.

As every good mother knows, you need to choose your battles. For some reason I decided in that moment that this was one worth fighting. With as much emphasis as I could summon, I pointed out what a shame it would be to not pursue a more worthy profession in his future. I explained there were ample octopus-like creatures already in the ocean, and that Mummy wasn't a fan of the sea in general so this wasn't really going to work for me. Now, the beauty of hindsight would suggest that trying to guilt-trip a toddler into changing his choice of future career into something I could brag about was not the best decision, but, hey, I didn't have the privilege of hindsight in the moment. William was undeterred… it seems the beauty of the underwater world had caught his eye. I am ashamed to admit I resorted to a somewhat less noble line of attack…. I decided to point out that the financial compensation for being a mollusc was not great. Yes, I played the salary card. 'Honey, I don't think you earn very many pennies being an octopus…'.

William looked at me aghast and stated 'But Mummy, you always said it doesn't matter how much money you earn, it's about doing what's in your heart!'. Humph.

If I'm honest, I'm not really a money motivated person. At the time I worked for a church, we don't tend to have that luxury! But in that one statement I realised how easy it is to forget about following your heart.

In that one slightly surreal conversation with my four year old I realised why Jesus said we should come to him as children. I think they have it right way more than we terribly grown up grown-ups do. They follow their dreams; they believe they can be anything they want to be (even if it's underwater sea creatures with slimy tentacles). They are not driven by money or status, they don't need to get their security or significance from their job - they simply want to do what is on their heart at that time.

The lesson to come like a child is one which has grown and morphed with me as my children have grown. They now sing at the top of their lungs. Are they any good? Frankly, no. They both sing out of time and in a key no one else has yet invented. Do they care? Absolutely not. They sing with abandon just because. Recently they have started writing songs. Unless the world goes totally nuts, these songs will never make it into the charts. Does that matter to them? No, it has never entered their heads that there is any need to compare what they do with what someone else does. They just write songs because they want to, it makes them happy. They paint and draw and dance and look at the world with an innocence of spirit which is like a breath of fresh air. They have not been tainted by the pressure to 'succeed' or the knowledge of the measures of success that are thrown at us by the world around us (which, for the record, are often not the same measures God would want us to use).

The conversation with William prompted me actually to step out into my dream of being a writer; I decided to follow my heart. I'm not going to be an octopus because they're ugly and slimy and I genuinely don't like the sea. When I announced it to myself and those around me it sounded terribly bohemian and ever so slightly self-indulgent; you see writing is what I love. It kind of feels like it shouldn't be the thing I get to do all day, it should be the thing I fantasise about whilst I'm folding the washing or cleaning the floor. (Just for the record – and specifically in case my husband is reading this – I do still clean floors and provide cleanish clothes). It's scary because it may not work and no-one may read what I write, or even worse they may read it and think it's awful; but for this next season I am going to follow my heart. I am going to try and become a little more childlike in my outlook and in my faith. I am going to try and get past the 'charts' and measures of success that would say there is a vast and wide chasm of possibility that this may fail compared to others.

To everyone who has ever asked a child 'What do you want to be when you grow up?' - keep asking that same question. Encourage them to believe that they can be anything they want to be. Then ask the same question of yourself. What do you want to be? What would you be if you only could? Push yourself to be a bit less grown up and sophisticated and find your inner child. Allow that child to push its way to the front, as only a child can. There's a reason Jesus told us to come to him as a child.

Pause and Ponder: I want to be an octopus

'In that one slightly surreal conversation with my four year old I realised why Jesus said we should come to him as children.'

What are the challenges to you of approaching your life and your faith like a child?

'To everyone who has ever asked a child 'what do you want to be when you grow up?' - keep asking that same question. Then ask the same question of yourself. What do you want to be? What would you be if you only could?'

Take a moment to ask yourself that question.

Yardsticks

When I was a child I sat down with my older brother to watch a game of rugby on TV. I was quite sporty as a kid and enjoyed football in particular, but rugby was new to me. I can remember my confusion as the player picked up the ball (not ok in football) and then threw it backwards down the pitch, when I would have suggested that throwing it forwards would have been a slightly more logical option. The most confusing part of the game was when the player ran as fast as his little legs would carry him to one end of the pitch before throwing himself into the mud whilst everyone celebrated - for some unfathomable reason a grown man face down on a muddy field hugging a strangely shaped ball seemed to be something worth awarding points to. Very confusing I can tell you.

The problem was that I didn't know what 'success' on a rugby pitch looked like. In other games I knew, picking up the ball and running down a field before throwing yourself on the floor would not have been a measure of success. It would have been a sign that medication was required.

It's important when you start playing a game, that you know what the point is before you start. Had I taken my football playing skills onto a rugby pitch, I wouldn't have done very well as the measure of success in the two sports is very different. Knowing your goal is an important way to help keep you motivated and a vital way of measuring success. Are you supposed to kick the ball into a net or pick up the ball and put it down over a line? If you keep on picking up the ball when you're supposed to kick it, you're going to struggle to succeed.

One piece of advice I live by is 'choose your yardstick carefully'. For you youngsters out there, a yard was what we counted in before metres were invented. A yardstick was a piece of wood with marks on it which gave you something to measure against. It was a measuring rod which gave a standard to use for comparison. It's so important to know what you are measuring your success against in order to know that you are measuring against the right thing.

In every area of my life I naturally compare myself to others. My clothes size, my parenting, my marriage, my writing, my abilities, my friendships... the list is endless. In my opinion, comparison is a killer; so many people are haunted by unhealthy comparisons. They choose terrible yardsticks to measure themselves against and always fail in their own eyes. Your waist line may not look like Victoria Beckham's but that doesn't mean you're a failure. Your marriage may not look like one from a rom-com but it doesn't mean it's not working. Your exercise regime does not need to rival that of an Olympian to help you get healthier. Choosing unrealistic or unhelpful yardsticks can be so damaging to your self esteem but also to the relationships and people around you. I know if I had always compared my husband to the characters in the latest film I'd watched, he would not be blessed by my measure of his success!

When it comes to achievement, we also need to choose our measuring stick carefully. If I expect my first ever book to make it onto the New York Times best seller list, and that is my only measure of success, I'm likely to be as disappointed as if I expect my waist line to look like Victoria Beckham's.

If we are choosing to pursue God sized dreams, we need God crafted yardsticks.

So many people trundle through life not having any goals or objectives. They neither succeed nor fail because there is nothing they are aiming for. I know in my work life that I have felt the most fulfilled, challenged and useful when I have had goals to aim for, deadlines to meet and measures of success to work at. If I don't have these, I become a strange mix of lethargy and procrastination. 'Failure' is hard but it often paves the way to success; never trying has to be the ultimate failure as there is nothing learned if nothing is ever attempted.

I have found that you need to be aware of your yardsticks in each area of your life. In order to be the best you that you can be, you need to be conscious about your measures of success and achievement or you'll either have wrong measures or no measures at all. Think of the rugby player. If he didn't know the aim of the game, how could he know if he had won, how would he know he had achieved anything?

There are so many things that shape our view of what is or isn't successful but God wants to be the one who helps us to craft and choose our yardsticks carefully.

In the current Western culture that I live in, the common yardsticks are fame and fortune. People are deemed to be successful by the size of their bank accounts or their twitter following. I live in a world where achievement is measured by salary, position and power. It is a place where a pop star has more impact on culture than a politician and where a 140 character sentence can shape the thoughts of millions in a matter of minutes. Don't get me wrong, influence is a good thing, if used well. Sadly, in the hands of many of the world's 'successes' it can be damaging and abusive in its effect.

It becomes second nature for people to feel worthless if they don't have the nice house and the nice car and the holiday and the clothes. If their phone is not the latest one available and their manbag or handbag doesn't contain at least one piece of clever technology. We measure ourselves by these things and can strive to achieve in order to simply get more and better stuff.

For the past five years I have been immersed in the world of church worship music. On a regular basis you end up questioning if you are doing well and your team is doing well. How do we measure up? Does anyone sing our songs? How many albums have we sold? What was the reaction to that new song on Sunday? Did people worship? Now, there can be benefits to asking these questions. It was my job to make sure that people felt our musical worship was good enough to engage with and that what we were producing was helpful and not distracting to their connecting with God. But all too easily the measures you live by slip to unhealthy comparisons of what someone else is doing and what another team has produced. Suddenly you are more concerned by a stranger's comments on your song than delivering what you feel God has put in your heart. Selling 2000 albums is about chart position rather than 2000 souls connecting with their Saviour. It is vital to be deliberate about your yardsticks and to keep checking your motivation against them.

Now that I have changed roles, I have to go through the process of figuring out my new yardsticks. It is human nature to want to succeed and I believe it is God's plan for us that we are successful in what we do, as long as we measure our success in the right way. Knowing my personality, I knew that I needed to figure out why I was doing this and what God wanted from me in order to know whether I was on track. Would I be doing well if I got a publishing deal or if a certain number of people bought my book? Would success be if I had a large number of blog followers or if people told me they loved what I had done? Well, all of those things would be nice but I knew from the outset that my ultimate yardstick had to be something else. If during the process of writing I got any of those things above, I could count them as blessings, but they couldn't be the reason for doing what I had chosen to do. Ultimately I had to go back to that initial dream that I had almost let go of. I wanted to use my words to reach people. I wanted others to know that there was someone who was walking through the same stuff that they were and asking the same questions of God, themselves and others. I wanted to create connections and cause people to think and I wanted to use the gift God had given me to draw people's eyes to His character and learn about Him. Keeping these things top of my list helps me to panic less when I write a blog post which next to no-one reads. I look back at it and ask the question 'Does it meet my yardstick?' Was it honest, did it glorify God, was it written to comfort and connect? If the answer to those is 'yes' then the fact that it didn't get thousands of hits seems less important. If I didn't have that yardstick I would analyse everything by numbers. I would write to an audience rather than writing from my heart. I would figure out which posts get more hits and engineer myself to be a people pleaser (which, believe me, is all too easy...). God hasn't called me to write niceties, he's called me to write about hope and truth. I have to trust that the right people will read my work, and if that is just one person, then that piece of writing is a success. It has achieved its purpose.

I love writing, most of the time, so I am getting to apply the majority of my time to a pursuit which energises and fulfills me. I like it, I want to do it, and I feel good having done it. For me, that is the first step in the right direction. Now I am not spoilt enough to think that you should always get to do what you love all the time, and believe me, there are moments when I want to throw my laptop through the nearest window, but I passionately believe that God wants us to enjoy the things we do. He doesn't want life to be one long hard drudge through a bog of mess that we hate. My understanding of God is that he wants us to live an abundant life. There are probably going to be times when we have to do jobs to pay the bills, whether we like it or not, but God has planted things in your heart that you love and that you are passionate about - He wants you to start watering and feeding those seeds. He says that He wants us to bear much fruit. In order to bear much fruit you need a decent sized tree.

You don't get fruit from an uncultured seed that sits dormant in the soil.

My husband works for a software company. He spends his days sorting out licenses and software agreements. There are times he enjoys his jobs and times he comes in from work needing to forget his day. His true passion, however, is music. He is one of the most talented musicians I have ever met. He is never happier than when he is sat in his little studio at home surrounded by instruments and recording equipment. He loves learning about new sounds and techniques, he enjoys crafting and composing music. At this time, his music does not pay the mortgage and so he balances provision and care for his family against using and pursuing his God-given talents. He is watering a seed whilst still putting food on the table. When David wrote the music I came down the aisle to, I didn't measure its success by how much money it brought in. It was the most amazing thing he ever wrote because of the heart it came from. He wrote that piece of music to tell a story and give a message. No one else in the world would need to even know that piece of music existed for it to be a success. If everything we produce or put our hand to is measured by fame and fortune, the real meaning behind it gets lost.

In the pursuit of our dreams we need to ask God what the yardstick needs to be. Don't let a useful tool become your yardstick. If you are an artist, ask yourself what you actually want from your art, what would you love people's response to be from what you have created? Take your fledgling plant to God and ask Him what He wants you to grow into and then keep on checking yourself against that stick. Don't let the temptations of the world over take your reason for stepping into your dream.

You see, I am finding that if you place God at the centre of your dream, He is likely to bless it in ways you never thought possible. God isn't interested in you becoming richer for the sake of it; if your motivation is purely financial, He's not going to give you anything that is bad for you. If you are creating something to simply be famous, I can't see Him moving heaven and earth for that cause.

I encourage each of us to look at our self. Look at what we are doing and ask ourselves the question 'what is my yardstick?' then go back on a regular basis and ask that question again and again. If your motivation starts to become something else, remind yourself of your measuring stick and throw anything else out.

I have never played rugby but from being married to a rugby fan I now know what the aim of the game is. I understand now why the player threw himself in the mud and why they often seem to be heading in the wrong direction. I know what their win is; I know how they are measuring success in their game. I have also learned to apply the analogy to myself. I need to know what the goal is, to know that my 'win' doesn't look the same as someone else's even if we're doing the same role. The truth is that being face down in the dirt can mean very different things depending on your yardstick.

Pause and Ponder: Yardsticks

'Choosing unrealistic or unhelpful yardsticks can be so damaging to your self esteem but also to the relationships and people around you.'

What yardsticks do you measure your success by? Are these helpful or damaging?

'He doesn't want life to be one long hard drudge through a bog of mess that we hate'.

How do you feel about this statement? Are there things you can do to change any drudgery in your life?

'God could trust me with it'.

Which things do you feel challenged to become more trustworthy with – money, public acclaim, opinion of others...?

Shepherds and sat navs

I'm not very good at following. I find people often walk just a little too slowly and I feel like I'm permanently about to step on their heels, so given the chance, and actually often even if I'm not given the chance, I choose to walk at the front of a pack. I like to set the pace, I like to figure out where we're going, I like to hold the map, I get impatient if people dawdle or stop to look at inane creatures or plants (I mean a plant is a plant right?). Basically, I'm not much fun to meander with but if you want to get somewhere quickly and efficiently, I'm your girl.

In life, as in nature, I'm impatient and terrible at being led. Awful! I'm realising that a life lived out with God is testing my natural desire to lead, set the pace, figure out the route, and generally be in control. Over the past few months I have found this an incredibly hard lesson to learn, and it has been the time when I have felt most challenged about whether I do actually trust God with my life or whether I'm perfectly happy to figure it out on my own, thank you very much.

This past September marked the time when both of my children would be in full time school. That gold-tinged day which I have secretly looked towards through the baby years of sleepless nights and endless nappies, and through the toddler time governed by tantrums, naughty stairs and early mornings. I didn't want to wish the time with the kids away but the day when they were both in full time school was the point on the horizon which signalled 'me-time', the opportunity to finally lose the baby weight and the first time in 6 years that I could visit the toilet on my own without 'help' or an audience.

I found in the months leading up to the start of school a heightened pressure to figure out the next stage, to know what God was calling me to do once the kids were at school. Should I carry on working at the church, or go back to teaching or something completely different? I decided to take some time out to ask God about the 'what next', to ask the big question of where I should be going, what job I should be doing, what role to put my hand to... To be honest I felt like I asked a million questions and got very few answers. The sort of guidance I needed seemed to fall into a grey area... there was no right or wrong, just one choice or another.

I think we probably all have situations which are the 'grey area' ones. The times where we need guidance and want to do the right thing or know the next step or the best way forward but there aren't specific verses in the bible which give us those answers. Because of this, I think the grey area questions are the really tricky ones. The bible is an amazing tool for God to speak to us about many things. He spells out the best way and then we have a choice to listen or to go our own way – don't steal, don't commit adultery, don't covet thy neighbour's ass even if theirs is a size 8 and yours is a size 14, but I am yet to find a verse saying 'and the Lord spake to his people saying 'leave thy current job to go and write that book you always wanted to'. I haven't found a verse which explains whether to buy a house or carry on renting, whether to move jobs, or leave your job altogether. It doesn't specifically say how best to use your time, where to serve at church, what role you're supposed to take in an organisation. It doesn't give me each and every detail of how best to step into my dreams and how to be the person I feel I was created to be. These 'grey areas' are where it can be so much harder to hear God's voice and to know his guidance. In fact my experience over those months was that, despite my asking, I came up with no answers, I felt like God was silent.

Why is that? The bible says that the Lord is my shepherd. Shepherds are supposed to guide us right? Why does it feel like I haven't received the guidance that the bible seems to promise me?

Well I realised quite late on in my seeking and questioning that I didn't actually want God to be my shepherd, I wanted him to be my

Satellite Navigation System. I love sat navs, they appeal to my personality - a little box which shows me the whole way, the whole time, the whole picture of how to get to my chosen destination. Genius!

I realised over this period of seeking God that I wasn't praying to Him as a shepherd, instead I had been praying sat nav prayers – how long will it take, where will I end up, how do I get there, am I going to hit any congestion on the way? I think we often want to have the whole journey planned out and shown neatly on a little screen attached to the front window. If I'm honest, I'd really like God to be one of the clever sat navs who can predict a difficulty and steer me round it, whose entire purpose is to get me from A to B in the least time, with the least amount of energy and certainly no inconvenience. I wonder if this sounds familiar? I wonder if you, like me, have ever found yourself questioning God because the path hasn't looked like the one you expected, if you've lost a little faith in God because your journey has not looked like the one you wanted? Have you ever found yourself asking sat nav prayers of where? And how? And how long? And what next? I am learning that the way of the shepherd is very different from that of the sat nav. If I'm honest it's been a tricky lesson to learn and I've had a few disappointments to contend with and a few difficult questions to ask but I think God has challenged me to ask the question 'do I trust God that a shepherd is better than a sat nav?'.

Firstly, I felt like I had to ask the questions "would I actually want to know everything that God knows about my journey and do I really want to be in control?".

Would I really want the whole journey plotted out before me on a little screen?

The more I looked back over my life, the more I realised how unhelpful it would have been to know what was coming up ahead. I think of the toughest of times. What would I have done if I had known they were coming? Well I guess the simple answer is that I would have avoided them at all costs. The deeper I thought about it, the more I realised that it was those things that have made me the person I am today. It was the things forged through the fire that were made of gold, it was because of walking through the flames that the chaff was burned out of my life. God knew what He was doing when he kept the path ahead from me. Would I have been better off knowing the route and what was ahead? Would I have led myself through any better than He did? Certainly not.

Even in the good times, the joy in the journey is the unexpected delight and the surprise encounters that lead to something unpredicted. Part of the wonder of life is the act of looking back and seeing each thread weave a beautiful picture that you never expected or thought possible. How dull to have all the answers in advance!

For sure it's appealing when you're in the confusion, but knowing the outcome of every venture or decision would certainly take the edge off every feeling associated with it, and dumb down every possibility for a lesson learned or a character shaped in the process.

A good shepherd

During this time of praying and seeking and trying to figure my next step out, I actually met a real shepherd. I happened to be at a friend's house for a summer barbecue and one of the other guests was a shepherd from New Zealand. I explained the fact that I was thinking about the analogy of God as a shepherd and he gave me some fascinating insights into the relationship of the sheep and the shepherd and the way that a good shepherd actually guides his sheep. He said that a good shepherd really does know his sheep, as the bible says that God knows us. He knows their personality, the best way to move them and encourage them, and when is the right time to give them a poke to get them going. He leads them according to their personality. There are those who are the leaders, always up the front and ready to go, who basically need a good firm hand and lots of space (that sounded pretty familiar...). Then there are the wanderers. Sheep that wander off don't just do it once and learn their lesson. Wandering sheep wander. And wander. And then wander again. The shepherd not only brings them back but expects to have to keep finding them and bringing them back. Then there are the ones lagging behind at the back, the sheep that need a bit more encouragement and a bit more help to keep going. The shepherd knows them and gives them that encouragement and support as they need it. The good shepherd treats each sheep as an individual.

The way of the shepherd is birthed out of relationship. *'The sheep know my voice, and they follow me'* (John 10:27). The shepherd knows the sheep and the sheep know the shepherd. The sheep don't expect to be handed a map or even be told which way to go, they simply stay close enough to hear and follow his voice wherever it leads them. They trust him.

This shepherd also told me that a good shepherd brings calm to the sheep. He knows that when the sheep are calm they move best, feed best and are led most effectively. If the shepherd is too loud, the sheep get skittish so he lowers his voice to a still small whisper to guide them. The shepherd brings calm and peace to the sheep; they trust that still small voice and then follow him where he leads them. Maybe the fact that God wasn't shouting my next step from the roof tops was indeed Him being a good shepherd; maybe the frustration with my future was not to be sorted by a detailed ten step plan of how to get to the next thing most effectively. Maybe I was supposed to be seeking a still small voice and learning how to follow such a whisper? Maybe I was supposed to be learning how to be a good sheep to the good shepherd rather than just worrying about the final destination?

A good sheep

If there was ever a good sheep, it was a guy called Abram. In the first book of the bible we read the story of Abram and his wife, a couple who went on to become the parents of God's people on earth. We read this in Genesis 12:1-4:

> 'The Lord had said to Abram, Go from your country, your people and your father's household to the land I will show you. I will make you into a great nation, and I will bless you; I will make your name great, and you will be a blessing. I will bless those who bless you, and whoever curses you I will curse; and all peoples on earth will be blessed through you. So Abram went, as the Lord had told him...'

I love the simplicity of Abram's faith. God said to him to leave everything he knew and loved and go somewhere un-named that He would tell him, at some undefined point in the future. And guess what? Abram went. Just like that. He heard, he trusted, he did what God asked. You'll notice God gives him a big picture of his future but absolutely no detail of what would happen along the way. For a control freak like me, that sounds like hell! I think back to the way I ask God to give me every minor detail about where and when and how and realise that the shepherd's way doesn't give those answers. He simply calls us to go the way He will show us. The sat nav prayers that I pray seek to get many details but the shepherd doesn't give me them; instead He gives me promises.

The reason Abram went was because he trusted God's promises over the detail of the journey. He didn't need to know the how or when because he knew the Who. His faith in the One who was leading was strong enough that he believed God would take him where he needed to go, in the way he needed to go, when he needed to go - he also knew that it was better that he himself didn't know!! What a challenge!

In my knotted journey of figuring out where I'm going, I realised that I was looking at all the wrong stuff and forgetting all the things I should be holding on to. If I really believe that God is faithful and kind, abounding in love, full of grace and truth, why on earth do I not trust Him with my future? Why do I so often question the path ahead? Why do I not trust Him that it is better for me not to have all the answers?

I ask myself the question again... Do I trust that a shepherd is better than a sat nav?

The problem with the sat nav way is that it appeals so strongly to me. I like to be in control, and I can be if I have it all plotted out in front of me. I am risk-averse, and the sat nav will help me avoid all the difficulties along the way. I want comfort and ease. I fear the unknown. I find trust difficult. Following a shepherd forces me to face these characteristics in myself and allows God access to dealing with them. Have you ever noticed that if you pray for patience you come across the most irritating individual you can imagine? When you pray for God to help you love more, you come across people who are super difficult to love. God doesn't dollop blobs of blessing down from heaven when he's trying to sharpen and teach you, he puts you slap bang in the middle of a situation that is going to exercise that muscle you want to grow. A word of advice - be careful what you pray for!

God doesn't do sat nav guidance

Stepping out in the 'grey area' decisions requires a shift of focus. Whatever decision is currently on your plate, you have options of how to face and deal with it. You can allow the fear, confusion, doubt, risk, need for answers and comfort guide your decision making or you can choose to fix your eyes on the one who can see the path you can't. We need to choose to shift our focus up.

In Isaiah 55:8-9, God says *'For my thoughts are not your thoughts, neither are your ways my ways' declares the Lord. 'As the heavens are higher than the earth, so are my ways higher than yours.'*

When we look up we have the opportunity to start on a trajectory that is higher than any one we could have come up with on our own. God doesn't do sat nav guidance because His ways are so far beyond ours that it would blow our minds. We would simply never be able to cope with the knowledge He has and so He gives us the detail we need at the right time. He is the one who knows what we can cope with, which is why He often only leads us one step at a time. Think back to Abram, all he needed to know was that he was supposed to leave home, then God would show him the details as and when he needed them. If you go on to read about Abram (who was later called Abraham) and the way his life went, you will see why it was best he didn't know it all at the beginning!

My four year old is currently in her first term at school. Last week we went to parents evening where they asked us to help her recognise two digit numbers. Now, as her parent I know that she can cope with that, just. I show her how to do the next thing she needs to in order for her to learn. Can you imagine how ridiculous it would be for me to give her quantum physics to work on? (Not that I could of course because I know about as much as she does about quantum physics.) It wouldn't help Megan, and neither would she understand it, if I gave her something which may be useful to her in twenty years' time but is way beyond what her mind can cope with now.

The most difficult thing to get our heads around is that there are times when God, in his infinite wisdom, chooses not to give us answers at all. Again, we need to choose to lift our eyes to Him and trust Him.

The second reason that God doesn't do sat nav guidance is because he is entirely concerned with your 'sheep-ness' (sure that's a word...). God is passionate about you being in relationship with Him and so he will never give you anything which negates your need for Him. The reason he guides as a shepherd is so that His sheep will stay close. If He chose to hand you a map or a detailed plan we wouldn't need to stay close enough to be able to hear His voice.

God loves you. Simple, profound, amazing truth. God loves you enough to want to guide you down paths of righteousness, into beautiful pastures and through the valleys when they happen. He wants you to live a life full up and flowing over, abundant and bountiful; He wants you to be fulfilled and live out your dreams. But do you know what he wants above all those things? He wants you. He wants you to be His before you are anyone else's. Wherever your feet tread and whatever the path ahead looks like, He is passionate about your sheep-ness, your belonging to Him. He doesn't love you more if you do follow His best path for you, He doesn't love you less if you simply sit down and refuse to move. He loves you because you are His sheep. You are His. Why would He give you anything that would pull away from that? He wants us to learn to be more concerned with our 'being' than our 'doing'.

I look back to the time where I sought God about the next stage of my life and realise that God seemed silent because I was asking questions which at the time He knew I didn't need the answers for. He was gently teaching me to spend time with Him because of who He is not because of what I can get from Him. If I spend more time and effort on my sheep-ness I am naturally going to be heading in the right direction because I will be with Him. If I can hear His voice I am in the right place because I am close to Him. It's also in this place that He is most likely to guide me because I will be able to hear the still small whispers about what to do next, about the best way to go, about the plan He has for my life.

In the pursuit of an extraordinary life, I think this is a lesson I will keep on coming back to. It challenges so many things at the core of my being, and it challenges the way I see God. Living a life that matters and has purpose will mean strange unexpected steps and odd detours. It will probably involve twists and turns I never thought would happen and opportunities I never expected. I'm so glad that I don't have to figure all of this out, but that I can trust it to a shepherd who loves me, and knows the best for me. My final lesson is to find joy in the journey, not just in reaching the destination. For me, writing books is a journey. At times, I just want to get the blasted thing finished so I can say to myself 'hoorah! You actually did it!'. But the beauty so far is how much I am being changed and challenged and blessed through the process. It makes handing control over to God so very much easier.

Thank God, the Lord really is my shepherd.

Pause and Ponder: Shepherds and sat navs

'The sort of guidance I needed seemed to fall into a grey area... there was no right or wrong, just one choice or another.'

Are you facing any grey area decisions?

'I realised over this period of seeking God that I wasn't praying to a shepherd, instead I had been praying sat nav prayers'.

What do your prayers resemble most closely - sat nav prayers or prayers to a shepherd?

'Do you trust that a shepherd is better than a sat nav?'

How easy is it to do this in your journey?

Fruit that will last

I am a terrible gardener. I kill every plant I am given, even if I really really try hard to keep it alive. I was bought a plant by a friend once which was labelled as 'unkillable'. I killed it. Green fingered I am not. But I am a grower. There's something in me which wants to help people to grow and achieve. If there's a way I can facilitate them believing they can be something, I will. I love to see people realise their potential and then meet it. I love to see faces light up when they realise something about themselves that they never knew before. I am a grower even if I'm not a gardener.

I don't know much about the process of growing plants, but I know they need nutrients and water, that they require light to grow, and that pruning makes for a better plant. I know that seasons are vital to plants and that even in the harshest of winters a plant is bedding down and recovering, ready to spring forth and produce fruit.

Producing fruit. That's really what it's all about isn't it? That's the whole point of a tree and it sums up that deep desire to do something with our lives... in order to produce fruit - something beautiful and life giving.

I can't tell which trees are which by their shape or leaves or size, but I can tell by their fruit. A tree covered in apples is, quite obviously, an apple tree. Even with my limited understanding of gardening, I'm able to figure that out. There are, however, a few apple trees out there who are trying to produce pears. Not actual trees of course, that would be ridiculous. But can I point out how equally ridiculous we can be in trying to be something we are not? The lure of someone else's fruit can sometimes cause us to try to change who we are and what God wants us to produce. If everyone produced apples, we would be much the worse off. If you're a pear tree, can I gently encourage you to work on growing the best pears you can rather than being a terrible apple tree? Don't fall into the age old trap of comparing your fruit with someone else's - it is never a positive exercise.

In the bible, God calls us to be people who produce much fruit, in fact he says that that is what He wants for us - that we are created to be 'much fruit' people. This promise is such an exhilarating one. And a challenge, of course, as many of God's promises are. You see, fruit production requires seasons, pruning, deliberate watering and feeding. It also requires time.

Through the hardest seasons of life, I am terrible for forgetting to stay fed and watered (not literally of course, or else I would be considerably more svelte than I am). I'm talking about spiritually.

When the going gets tough, I tend to roll in a ball and whine gently and irritatingly to myself and anyone else who will listen. It is during the hard seasons, when the work is going on deep underground, that we need to stay fed and watered or we won't be able to produce the fruit we could in the next season.

I have a friend who is an up at dawn bible reader. She makes herself a coffee and every morning sits and feeds herself on God's sustenance. She even has a head torch for the winter months. Brilliant. She has a good relationship with her spiritual food. She eats when hungry and drinks when thirsty. My spiritual diet is a little different. I'm more of a binge eater. I don't mean to be but I've never got my head around the head-torch at dawn routine. I tend to eat and eat one day and then starve myself for several days, wondering why I have no energy or get up and spiritual go. Luckily I have good friends who help me to eat better. They encourage me, and send me emails with bible verses and God truths. We meet weekly and dig into ideas on faith - they basically help me not to starve myself for too long. It has been in the winter seasons that I have needed to keep feeding and watering myself so that I have any hope of being a 'much fruiter'. I am so pleased I get to be a fruit tree in an orchard of other such trees. I'd be a useless tree on my own.

It has also been invaluable to be doing this journey with others when the pruning happens. The times when something is lopped off with a great big axe which leaves you feeling a little sore and like you're literally missing a limb. I have been amazed at what has been pruned over the years, but nothing amazed me more than when something good was hacked off. When you've given yourself to something, something good and worthwhile, when you've poured your whole self into it and that is pruned. Ouch! I mean the grotty stuff, although a bit painful, I can understand. When God prunes my negative attitude or selfishness, I get that, but when he prunes the thing I thought I was all about, that's trickier. Sadly, even the best branches that once produced much fruit will at some point need to be cut off. That branch you were most proud of, that in the past was your mega fruit producer, probably won't be for ever. In order to keep on producing fruit, some branches that you relied on in the past need to be pruned in order for others to be given the chance to produce more. It hurts but ultimately it's worth it if we want to keep producing fruit year after year, and season after season. How awful to be an old withered tree, clinging on to one old withered, past its best branch, when with a bit of trimming and re-shaping we could have been a vibrant, fruit bearing success.

God not only calls us to produce much fruit, but to produce fruit that will last. Money, recognition, power, acclamation will all fade. God wants us to have better fruit than these things. Some fruit is unpalatable, others taste good for a while but can ultimately make us sick. God wants us to produce fruit that will sustain, that will last beyond ourselves, that will make a difference and leave a mark on those who see it and taste it.

What on earth does this fruit look like? What sort of fruit should I be producing?

> *'But the fruit of the Spirit is love, joy, peace, forbearance, kindness, goodness, faithfulness, gentleness and self-control.'* Galatians 5:22.

These are the fruits God wants us to produce: His fruits. These are the fruits that will make a difference in His kingdom, that will sustain a broken world that is crying out for food to stop the hunger pains; that will fill them up so they won't go hungry any more. These are the seeds we should be watering in order to produce orchards of His grace. These are the things He sows in us, then wants us to grow in order to feed those around us.

When God says He wants us to produce much fruit, this is the fruit He is talking about. When He crafted you in your mother's womb, when He dreamed you up in heaven before you were even considered on earth, these were the things He planted deep inside you and these are the things He wants you to produce. This is why He calls you to step out and dream big, because the world is crying out to be fed and you are just the right tree to produce just the right fruit to feed them.

Through your words and actions, your time and gifting, through using the things he wove into you deliberately, you can be a 'much fruiter' that can sustain the hungry and feed the starving. You can show a glimpse of the God of the universe through your fruit because He is the vine we are all attached to. He is at the centre of it all. It flows from Him, and is sustained by Him. He gives you all you need to produce the fruit embedded deep within you which the world is crying out for.

I think God is willing you on to believe Him that he has made you to produce much and lasting fruit. His pruning, His watering, His feeding, His growing you and shaping you has been for one purpose; so you will produce all you are capable of producing.

As I write, I am looking out onto my garden. It is a child and dog friendly functional garden. It has grass and shrubs that cannot be damaged by footballs and over excited puppies. It's growing, it's alive, but it has no beauty - it is simply functional.

I went for years being a shrub. Hardy, ready to survive the elements. I had toughened up over time so that I couldn't be broken or battered too hard. I was alive, yes, but there was little beauty to what I produced, I was simply functional. It was a bleak existence.

God wants to take your brittle shrub and transform it into something vibrant, beautiful and life giving. Something that can feed and sustain others, something that draws attention and is thriving whatever the season.

He is taking a generation of functional shrubs and calling us to become trees of His righteousness, planted by His streams of living water that will not wither and will not die. He is creating a beautiful orchard and He wants your unique tree to be a part of that.

Pause and Ponder: Fruit that will last

'I know that seasons are vital to plants'.

What season are you currently in - at home, at work, in your family, in your friendships? What are the benefits and difficulties of this season?

'Don't fall into the age old trap of comparing your fruit with someone else's.'

Is this something you struggle with? How does this affect your journey?

'In order to keep on producing fruit, some branches that you relied on in the past need to be pruned in order for others to be given the chance to produce more.'

Have you ever had to go through a season of pruning? How did this feel and how do you learn to walk that season well?

'This is why He calls you to step out and dream big, because the world is crying out to be fed and you are just the right tree to produce just the right fruit to feed them.'

What fruit do you have or could you have that the world is crying out for?

'He is creating a beautiful orchard and He wants your unique tree to be a part of that.'

Do you have faith that your 'tree' is both unique and vital?

Underdog

In Britain, we love the underdog. Generally, we struggle to support those who start off on top, the privileged, the blessed and the naturally gifted, and as a nation we probably need to learn to encourage them too rather than knock them down or find fault, but we do love a good underdog story. I think it's because we're so small; geographically I mean. You'd think Britain covered half the world, the way we talk about ourselves, when actually we're a bit of a pimple on the backside of mainland Europe. I like that about us though; we do what we can with what we have and we're not doing too badly all in all. We do have a bit of a tendency to turn up to other countries, stick a flag in them and declare them ours, which is a little presumptuous. I do apologise to anyone out there if we tried to stick a flag in you, it's because we're small and surrounded by sea... there's not really anywhere else for us to go. We are not a nation who takes things lying down, we like to take on the big boys, and we do so love the underdog.

So many of the inspiring stories of people in the bible and so many of the people who inspire me today are extraordinary despite humble beginnings or difficult situations The underdog stories are the ones that stir my soul and cause me to believe it possible for me to be someone who could make a difference. It's the people who overcome adversity and who achieve greatness despite hardship who we cheer on most strongly and it's the ones who are surprisingly extraordinary who lift us most.

Take Esther, an average girl whose story is slotted into the middle of the bible between kings and champions. Esther was a Jewish orphan living in exile, adopted by her cousin; on paper she was not destined for greatness. Hoorah for others of us who are nothing on paper! What did Esther have to start with? Well, she had little more than a pretty face. It's not much to work with is it? I mean, she'd be fine if she entered Miss World but it doesn't really seem like the best way to achieve greatness and have a lasting impact on the world.

To me, Esther is the ultimate underdog, and I love her for it. You see if she was born into royalty, born a man, born a leader, it would change the way you would cheer-lead her on the path that she trod; but her humble beginnings, her gender and her lack of prospects just highlight how incredible her amazing influence really was.

The lesson of Esther has to be one of using your influence for good - wherever you are. When she was placed in a massive spa ready to be pimped out to a not very nice king, she was kind and found favour. She influenced those around her well. If you look back at her story, she doesn't even seem to have had an option about where she ended up, her cousin put her forward for the nationwide beauty contest with the grand prize of being married to an unpleasant tyrant who disposed of his last wife. Not a nice guy and not an enviable position to find yourself in. Her beauty started her on the road she walked but her true beauty was not found by looking in a mirror, but rather by looking beneath the surface to her character.

Esther didn't wait until she was in a better position before she used her influence for good. She did it in the tough times; she did it wherever she went. Esther did not always influence kings, she started off influencing eunuchs, but that did not change who she was, she used her influence well in each situation she found herself in. Everyone has influence somewhere and over someone. It may not be who you would like but you have an option as to what sort of influence you have wherever you go. Throughout the story of Esther, she leaves positive fingerprints on every life she touches. What do you touch? What in your day to day life do you handle? Who are you leaving fingerprints on? And what sort of impression are you leaving?

Being a good influence is not about being a people pleaser, but it is about leaving godly touches wherever we go and on whoever we meet on our path. I hope that wherever I go, I leave positive marks; I hope people are pleased when I walk into a room rather than look for the nearest exit. I have a choice about what sort of influence I have on the people around me, and it's often done with the words I speak and the way I treat the people I come across.

Esther progressed to the top not by having an agenda or a plan, but rather by using her influence well.

I don't know about you, but I find people with an agenda hard to warm to. You can figure them out straight away. It's often those who aren't happy where they currently are and who can be found trying to claw their way up the nearest ladder. These people tend not to be content unless they have a title or a role, and often seek after 'leadership' like a kid after a chocolate bar with no consideration for those around them. They leave a trail of hurt and sadness behind them as they trample their way to the place they feel they deserve to be in.

I believe that God calls and equips people for leadership, but the best leaders that I have ever met are those who have simply led wherever they are and influenced the people round them well in whatever role or situation they have found themselves in. Very often, the doors have then opened to other opportunities and responsibilities on the back of this. The people who don't seem to care about role or title are often the best ones to hold them.

A wise friend once told me that you aren't a leader because you receive the title of it; you're a leader when people follow you.

I think Esther epitomises this. She didn't need to go to leadership seminars, she had no role or title to start with, because of the culture she lived in a woman could have no agenda, she just influenced the people round her well and the doors opened.

One of my favourite moments in the story of Esther comes when she finds herself in a position of being able to influence the king. She wins his favour and becomes his wife, and then finds out about a plot to slaughter the Jewish people. She invites the king and the man responsible for the fate of her nation to dinner. Now, had that been me, I would have prepared a moving speech in order to show the king the error of his ways, I would probably have rushed in with passion and maybe the odd tear demanding justice. Esther says nothing. She bides her time and uses her words sparingly. Oh the challenge for the extroverts amongst us!

Sometimes, the right thing for us in a given situation is to say nothing. Sometimes the best way to influence those around us is through restraint and wisdom rather than by constantly voicing our opinions on any poor soul that will listen. Influence is sometimes silent, but other times calls us to stand up with valour and say the tough thing. Esther did both - most importantly, she knew how and when to do both. She knew when to speak, she honoured the king as he was her leader even when he didn't deserve it, she knew when to hold her tongue and she used all she had to further God's plan. She chose to act beyond herself and to put herself in harm's way for the sake of the greater good. What an amazing example of influence and leadership.

Esther's famous words, that maybe she was in the position she was 'for such a time as this' are scaffolded by a character of true integrity and amazing influence. The underdog, the woman, the orphan, who goes on to save a nation, is one of my greatest inspirations because of this.

At such a time as this, where do you find yourself? Maybe, like Esther, it's not somewhere you thought you would be, maybe you are facing an unenviable task, maybe you're stuck in a spa with a eunuch, unlikely, but good luck to you if you are. Our lives are a catalogue of opportunities to impact people positively in a wide variety of scenarios, and we never know where any opportunity or situation may lead. I believe we are called to accept where we are, just at this time, and use where we are, the hand dealt to us to bring God's character to those around us. We can never second guess God's plan or try to engineer ourselves to be where we want to be rather than where we have been placed, we can simply be the best we can be right where we are.

Esther's story encouraged me to stop looking to the next thing and use what I have where I am for the glory of God and the benefit of those around me. It stopped me buying into the lie that only 'leaders' have influence and helped me to realise that the people we should be influencing are already around us. Whether we like it or not, we all leave evidence of where we have been. If you aren't conscious, those marks of your presence may not be the best marks that they could be. In always looking for the next thing, you can miss the reason you are where you are.

Esther's extraordinariness was not in her role, but in her character; it was in her untitled state that she learned how to use her title well when it came to her. The integrity she showed before she was the Queen was what led her to being the best Queen she could be, and this ultimately put her in the history books.

In the West, we live in a world of social media and connectedness. Unlike ever before, every person has the opportunity to have influence and there are so many examples of 'unknowns' trending on twitter, becoming a huge youtube phenomenon, but public fame is not on everyone's path. It is the conversation in the school yard or the chat over a coffee at work which can have influence in ways we never expected and could never predict. You don't know who is watching you, who sees your life and is either inspired or turned off by it. People look at us all the time to see what we are doing and to learn from our actions. If you are a Christian, people will also be looking at you to see what faith looks like in the flesh, they will look at the way you speak about others, how you parent, whether you stick to the morals you profess to have. If they want to know what faith is all about, you are the one they will look to to start figuring it out. This shouldn't be a pressure on us, rather a tremendous opportunity to be that positive influence, to show Jesus to the world around us. As I said at the start of this book, you don't need to quit your life in order to be something extraordinary - you simply need to live it well. The most amazing ways to start making a difference in the world around you are to show kindness, love, generosity, acceptance; to show the characteristics of Jesus which drew crowds to Him.

The bible tells us that where much is given, much is expected. In so many ways, every one of us has been given so much. We often compare 'up' to the people with more - more money, more influence, more responsibility, a better house or car or job; but compared to so many you will be a 'much' person. In the West, financially we are 'much-ers', just hop on a plane to many other less fortunate, less stable nations to learn that lesson. We have been given much; food, cars, support, health care, political freedom. We have an awful lot of much. As Christians, we have been given even more than these things. We have been handed a tray of much blessing, much grace, much mercy and love, much forgiveness, much joy, much peace.... I could go on and on. Suffice it to say that much has indeed been given. On top of that you have been given specific gifts, experiences and traits which are part of the tray of much that God refers to in the bible. The second part of that verse therefore applies to us - much is expected.

I encourage you not to compare your much with someone else's much, it's very dangerous. It has a habit of pulling us into envy and jealousy. The truth for each of us is that God knows you so very well, down to the hairs on your head. He sees the 'much' you, the much you can handle, and what your much looks like. He didn't give you what your neighbour has or what your friend has because he wants you to have what you have. The much expected He wants from you comes from the much given He has already lavished upon you. He doesn't expect you to summon anything up with nothing to start with; all that you need has already been bestowed on your head.

There is a call to step up; there is an expectation on you. Not a pressure, I hasten to add because Jesus clearly taught that as gifts were apportioned, so the return is expected. He doesn't expect something we cannot deliver, but He does expect. He expects us not to hide our light, it is there to shine; He expects us to love Him and others because He is in us and He is love; He expects us to use the talents we have been given, that's why they are there. How sad to have been given talents and to let them rot or go to waste, often accompanied by a complaint that God never uses us or that we are no good at anything. Everyone has something they can use and something they can bring to the table - our table needs your talent in order for the feast to be complete.

You may think what you can offer is small or useless - don't believe it! Your talent may not be as obvious as someone else's, it doesn't matter. You may not be a shining star, God needs your star anyway; He is the one who will make it shine. Once we start to use what we have in the place we currently find ourselves, God will open up the door for new opportunities where we can grow and sharpen our gifts. Look back at Esther's story; she used her gifts in the unnoticed opportunities and then God opened a way for her to offer them on a more public stage. He knew she had exercised that muscle and could handle the pressure of something more public; after she had been faithful in the small; she was trusted with more.

This is a note to the underdogs. You may be looking at yourself thinking 'What on earth do I have to offer?'. You may struggle to see how you could bring anything of any worth or see how you could make any difference with what you have in your little basket of gifts; I encourage you to sit down with a good friend and ask them to help you to figure out what you have. I promise you, there will be something there that someone is crying out for. It can be hard to know ourselves at times, I am specifically bad at this. It took me a lot of time, a lot of conversations with people I trusted to be able to figure out me - not the roles I did but the person God created me to be. When you can't see it in yourself, sometimes you need to ask someone you trust what they can see in you. The better you know yourself, the more easily you will be able to pull something out when you face someone who needs something. All the much that is in you is going to waste if you don't know it's there or if you are afraid to pull it out of your basket. There will be someone in your world who is crying out for you - someone who needs a friend, who needs help with their marriage, who needs company, who needs a meal or some money; they may need your words or your prayers or your encouragement or your kindness. I don't know what it is for you specifically, but can I encourage you to know what you have so that when someone in your world needs something, you know you have it there to offer?

You have the capacity to influence the happiness, the well being, the soul of another person. You have the capacity to lead them by your example, for good or for ill. You have the capacity to meet the practical need of someone in your street as well as someone on the other side of the world. You have a huge capacity, and your willingness to use and grow that capacity is the thing that greatness is made of. I pray you don't allow yourself to live as an underdog, don't allow the things of your past or your present to steal your opportunity to use the much you have been given. You may not have

104

started with much; you may feel like the Jewish orphan girl with little to offer the world and few prospects which the world would rate, but maybe down your path is the possibility that you could change the world, if only you are faithful with your much right now, right where you are.

Pause and Ponder: Underdog

'What do you touch? What in your day to day life do you handle? Who are you leaving fingerprints on? And what sort of impression are you leaving?'

How do these questions apply to your life?

'The lesson of Esther has to be one of using your influence for good – wherever you are'.

Where are you and who are you influencing right now?

'At such a time as this, where do you find yourself?'

Are you where you thought you would be at this stage in your life? How can you use the place you are currently at to its fullest?

'Esther's extraordinariness was not in her role but in her character'.

What character traits could you be working on now? Are there things you need to be strengthening?

'The much expected He wants from you comes from the much given He has already lavished upon you'.

What 'much' do you have? Maybe sit with someone else to work out your strengths and gifts if you aren't sure about what you have to offer the world around you.

Shadow sides

Have you ever noticed how the thing that caused you to like a person initially, is the thing that, in time, drives you crazy about them?

This is no better illustrated than in the marriage relationship. I tread carefully here as my husband is the introverted sort who feels no need to share his every experience with the whole world, say in his wife's book. In order to honour him, as I am clearly instructed to do, I shall change all names to protect anonymity.

Let's just say, for instance, that somebody has a husband called... say, Joe. Joe is a kind, introverted soul. He is committed to his friends and family, is popular and successful at work, he is confident and comfortable in his own skin. He has a high self esteem but not in a boastful arrogant way; he is firmly rooted and is not swayed by public opinion; he is a family man and has been brought up to want to provide for his wife and kids - he takes that role seriously. He is quietly loving, not overly so in the 'public displays of affection' which we all know can be a bit gag-worthy, and he is an amazing musician (Joe, that is) - he loves to create music and play with ideas and often produces something quite beautiful.

What a man this ~~Dave~~ Joe is! You can hardly believe his wife would think him anything other than perfect. Fast forward five years, two toddlers, endless sleepless nights, 10kg in weight (her not him) and a new puppy that has no discretion over where she goes to the toilet.

'Joe' walks in from a long day at the office providing for his family ('You're late again!! Your dinner's in the dog! You don't care!'), he greets them in his quietly loving way ('You never kiss me like they do in films! Why do married people never kiss just for the sake of it?') and gets changed before dinner (which she prepared, and will probably be complained about by at least one family member, just for the record - in this hypothetical situation...).

When the kids are in bed he takes himself off to his ~~Dave Cave~~ studio to work on some music ('He's always in that room tinkering on his music, you'd think he was single with no responsibilities and no washing up to do... and don't get me started on the fact that the skirting boards have not been completed 18 months later'), before spending a few (long) hours listening to his wife talk about her day ('You'll never guess what she said.../What do you mean you don't care?.../Are you even listening?...'). He has promised a friend that he will help him with a DIY job ('Maybe you could finish the skirting boards before you sort someone else's house out?') because he is the kind, committed sort who likes to help out.

All joking aside, so many relationships are affected negatively by the things which used to be the strengths. Each positive trait has a shadow side. A husband's strength of character can become stubbornness, a friend's happy-go-lucky nature can cause insecurities, a boss's leadership style can become like a noose round your neck. Every trait has a shadow side, every talent and dream can have a shadow side too.

Imagine the perfect life. What would it look like? People, places, opportunities, successes. What job would you be doing? Where would you be living? Who would it be with? Even if you got all of this, there would be a shadow side.

Ask any Mother what it's like being a parent. She'll tell you the amazing parts and if you push a little deeper, she'll give you the shadow side. (If she's in the thick of it, you may not have to push very deep at all to get the shadow side!) Ask anyone who has been married, anyone in your chosen profession, anyone who is living a dream like yours - there will be amazing moments and those same things will have a negative side too.

The dream of being a writer is an amazing picture for me - freedom, time to write on your own, no office politics to contend with, time to explore your creativity, time to do what you love. On the flip side, it can be insanely lonely, just you and your laptop - so much that you crave the office politics in order just to speak to another human being. Freedom can quickly morph into indiscipline and lethargy; creativity can dry up and what you loved can easily become a huge weight. You can quite quickly get to the point where any other job in the world sounds appealing.

I'm quite certain that if you speak to anyone who is living out their dream job or lifestyle, they will tell you that it is not all a bed of roses. Sometimes we fall into the 'if only's' - a very dangerous place to live.

If only my husband or kids were more like yours, if only I had that house, if only I went to that church, if only I did this job - then my life would be perfect. The truth is, your life would never be perfect... not this side of heaven at least. I don't say any of this to stop you dreaming - that wouldn't fit terribly well in this book, now would it? I say it because suddenly discovering a shadow side can create a chasm that can swallow you up if you aren't expecting it. Wherever possible, we need to go into things with our eyes wide open. We need to be wise; we will then stand a better chance of negotiating the chasm and living out the dream well.

We can choose to see the good or we can allow ourselves to focus on the bad; we can decide to make the best of our situations, or we can only look at the negative and fall into a pit of disappointment and negativity. These shadow sides burst the bubble. This can either cause us to give up, or force our hand on how we are going to deal with the darker side of the situation. I can either accept that being a writer can be lonely and frustrating at times or give up and do something else. I can learn to live with the more fluid nature of my dream or allow it to affect the outcome of my future.

When we start to witness the shadow side, we can either gird our loins or fall by the wayside.

The bible says we are in a battle. This battle is the culmination of the story of God going out to rescue back His family to Himself. There is an enemy that would come to kill and destroy, to stop people finding a God who loves them, who would stop them from having a life of fulfillment and promise, an enemy who desires to steal their joy.

So often, we allow the enemy to do just that. We give in so very easily because our reality has another side that we weren't expecting. God calls you to take your place in this battle, we each have a unique role given to us. He has gifted you and prepared you for the role He wants you to take in His rescue mission. You have the talents, the opportunities, the situation you need to be what He wants you to be. You also have a choice. You can choose to push through the shadow sides, to persevere, to look for the good instead of focusing on the bad - or you can give in and give up.

Let's go back to Joe.

His introverted nature, his strength of character, his desire to provide for his family, his commitment to help out his friends, his need for the Dave Cave (!!!) can be the things that make or break his marriage depending on how they are seen and how they are adapted to.

There have been times in our marriage, when Dave and I have had to really work at getting through the tough times. On many, if not all, of these occasions, I can look back and see that we were choosing to look at the shadow side of each other's personality or the situation we found ourselves in rather than trying to remember the good side of the same thing. It is good for me to remember why Dave may be late in from work every now and again - I choose to thank God that he is willing to work hard so that I can be a penniless bohemian writer. When he needs his own space, I have an option of what my attitude to that will be - do I resent his need for time on his own or graciously allow him to be who God created him to be?

I have had to apply the same lesson to so many areas of my life. When my children wouldn't sleep, I learned to thank God that I had children; some people will never have the blessing of a child, awake

113

or asleep. When a friend let me down, I had to choose to see the good in them, even when it was hard. When a door closed in my face, I learned to accept that it was for the best even if it hurt and left splinters in my nose. When I am frustrated with my writing or am feeling lonely, just me and my laptop, I choose to be grateful that I am in a period in my life when I get to do the thing I love most. It's all about how you choose to see something.

In the same way that everything has a shadow side, every cloud also has a silver lining. You may be in a position you don't want to be in. You may be frustrated that things don't look like what you thought. Maybe you've tried to make things happen but they just aren't working out quickly enough, or even at all. I encourage you to find that sliver of silver. It will be there somewhere. Whether it's a work issue, a relational one, a desire that won't be fulfilled, a dream that just won't come about - seek the silver. God promises He will never give us more than we can handle, He also promises that He has your path mapped out. You are where you are for a reason. You can either look at the shadow side or choose to live in the silver lining.

Pause and Ponder - Shadow sides

'Every trait has a shadow side, every talent and dream can have a shadow side too.'

Think about your personality. What are your best traits, your greatest talents, your wildest dreams - can you think what the shadow sides to these may be? How can you learn to bring out the best not the worst?

'Sometimes we fall into the 'if only's'.

Is this something you struggle with in any area of your life?

'You can either look at the shadow side or choose to live in the silver lining.'

Are there aspects of your life where you need to seek the silver lining, choose to see the positive rather than focusing on the negative?

Filters

I find the concept of 3D glasses intriguing. Now I have to admit to being a total technophobe so I'm thinking of the old style green and red glasses rather than the super cool looking new version. How is it that two coloured bits of film can make you see something in a completely different way? How does it recreate the view in front of us? The thing with 3D films and pictures is that if you aren't looking through the right filter, all you see is a fuzzy distorted version of what you should be seeing. I believe the same can be said about the way we look at ourselves and our identity. We live life looking through filters and for many people this gives us a distorted view of what we should be seeing, a view that is very different from how God sees us.

In the Book of Judges in the Old Testament, we come across a man named Gideon. Gideon was an Israelite, one of God's chosen nation, but at the time when Gideon lived, his people were under fierce attack from two neighbouring nations and Gideon was called by God to attack one of them and free his people. Gideon went on to win an amazing battle and drew the Israelites back to God.

It's really interesting to me to compare the Gideon at the start of the story to the triumphant man of God at the end. When we first come across Gideon, the Israelites were scared and were hiding out in dens and caves for protection. God sends a messenger to Gideon to tell him to stand up and make a difference but Gideon lacks faith, he finds it difficult to reconcile the assurances of God to his current situation. We read in Judges 6:12-16:

'When the angel of the Lord appeared to Gideon, he said, 'The Lord is with you, mighty warrior.' 'Pardon me, my lord,' Gideon replied, 'but if the Lord is with us, why has all this happened to us? Where are all his wonders that our ancestors told us about when they said, Did not the Lord bring us up out of Egypt? But now the Lord has abandoned us and given us into the hand of Midian.''

The Lord turned to him and said, 'Go in the strength you have and save Israel out of Midian's hand. Am I not sending you?' 'Pardon me, my Lord, 'Gideon replied, 'but how can I save Israel? My clan is the weakest in Manasseh, and I am the least in my family.'

The Lord answered, 'I will be with you, and you will strike down all the Midianites, leaving none alive.'

When we first meet Gideon, he is looking at himself through a filter. He has the filter of guilt, negative past history, lack of faith and huge self esteem issues covering his view of the future. Even when God speaks to him directly and gives him personal promises and assurances, Gideon cannot see himself as God does, he still looks through a filter of doubt.

I know so many people who struggle to reconcile the assurances God has put on their lives even if they feel God has communicated to them directly. It is possible to have been a Christian for many years, to serve faithfully and be seen to be doing all the right things, and still struggle to see ourselves clearly as God sees us. I think the problem is to do with filters. If we have the wrong filter, the wrong set of glasses on, we end up seeing everything around us as a poor, fuzzy version of what it actually is and what God means it to be.

These filters look different for different people. Some people are stuck with glasses of disappointment; their lives filtered by promises which have yet to come to fruition. Others look at their world through filters of abuse or brokenness. Many people allow negativity or comparison to colour their view. The list goes on and on.

The problem with these filters is that we often don't know we are looking through them because what we see is what we are used to seeing. The view is 'normal' even if it is not right. I went for a very long time looking through a filter of poor self esteem. I felt constantly out of my depth, comparing myself to the people around me and always coming off worst. I looked at the things in my world and saw all of them as a hindrance - my age, my size, my gender, my abilities or lack of them. Even if someone spoke positively into my life I'd find a reason to doubt that God could use me in any way. I had such a small view of myself and my capabilities that I would even hold myself back when opportunities arose, assuming I'd somehow mess them up or make a fool of myself. Like Gideon, I often felt like the least of the least. But God didn't want Gideon to look at himself through a dodgy filter, and he didn't want me to either.

God's promise to Gideon was that He would be with him. That he would win the battle in front of him because of God's presence rather than anything else which needed to change in Gideon. This is the key to the change of filter. We simply need to recognise God's presence with us in all that we face. His Spirit is with us and we are not expected to do anything in our own strength, but through His. God calls us to do all things in His strength - all things! The big, the small, the mundane, the extraordinary. ALL THINGS! That's quite a promise to give to us, that God is interested in everything and He will power us through all things.

Understanding God's strength and His ability as well as His view of each of us is the key to smashing those glasses that distort our perspective.

Any filter from your past or present that holds you back needs dealing with. It takes wisdom to know the filters are there and wisdom to know how to deal with them - but God wants you to know you can face your battles, as He wanted Gideon to know. Don't live with the lies that hold you back and keep you afraid of achieving your goals - lies that you are too old, or too young, that you can't if you're single or that you're held back if you're married. You are neither 'too' anything or 'not enough' anything for the road God has before you. You are just the right fit. Don't let anything paralyse you into inaction.

The only filter we need to look ahead with is that our God is greater; and that if He is with us, we can be greater too. God is greater than the lie you tell yourself, than your situation, than your hurts and disappointments. You may say, well that's all well and good for you, but you don't know my situation. And you'd be right, I don't. The truth is your situation may be awful, and it may not change - I don't know what lies ahead for you; but I do know God can change the way you look at your situation and the way you look at your life.

Maybe the very thing which is currently holding you back is the somehow part of the plan.

When God taught me to take off the filters, it was not a harsh lesson of God wanting to discipline me, it was a gentle encouragement to realise my potential and to be able to look at myself with clarity for the first time. I wonder if He is coming to you with the same encouragement? Whether He wants gently to slip off the glasses which have warped and distorted and held you back and instead open your eyes to how much He loves you and the amazing plan He wants you to step into? Maybe instead of disappointment and lack of faith He is offering you hope and restoration and healing and forgiveness.

Imagine if we really saw ourselves as God does, as someone worth the death of His Son, as someone who has been given amazing talents and gifts to live an amazing life for His glory. This is the God who goes to the man who is the least of the least and asks him to change the future of a nation. This is the God who causes broken souls to see lives of purpose and promise, where those whose dreams have never been fulfilled can achieve incredible things despite their disappointments. God doesn't want you to go through life seeing a poor fuzzy version of yourself but instead to see the amazing, multi-coloured, multi-dimensional life that He calls you to step into.

Pause and Ponder: Filters

'We live life looking through filters and for many people this gives us a distorted view of what we should be seeing, a view that is very different from how God sees us.'

Are there any filters which you are looking at yourself through, things from your past or present, which differ from what the bible says about you?

'I know so many people who struggle to reconcile the assurances God has put on their lives even if they feel God has communicated to them directly.'

What promises has God spoken over your life? Are there assurances or promises of God that you struggle to reconcile to yourself or your situation?

Snowflakes

Today it started to snow. At first there were barely-there wisps which hung in the air like a cold promise, then tiny snow drops started to fall and before long the sky was white and the ground was following suit. There's something very graceful about snow. I mean both in the way it dances to the ground, which is beautifully graceful, but also the grace found in the blanket that a good snow fall creates on the greyest of grounds. Snow covers a multitude of dirt and grime and ugliness, silently and gently, flake after flake until all that can be seen is gleaming white.

That is until my children descend upon it, turning it into a grey mush which will harden into an icy death trap.

When I was breast feeding my son, I would often pause on my midnight slumber-filled walks to his room, and look out of the window at the stillness of the night outside. There was something surreal and otherworldly about the times when it had snowed. There was a glimmer to the whole silent scape that I could see; it was like someone had whitewashed everything, with only me to behold it.

Some days I feel like a tiny insignificant snowflake. Just one little fleck falling through the sky, without much design as to where I am heading. One snowflake doesn't mean much, one snowflake doesn't make much impact, just like one drop of water or one grain of sand doesn't. We can look at our snowflake, our tiny grain or droplet, and ask ourselves what difference we can make, certainly when we see such an expanse of dirty grey world before us. Sometimes the fight just seems too big, the mountain too high, the task too mammoth for our little selves to make any difference.

There *is* a dirty grey world out there - ridden with corruption and poverty and sadness and disease. It is a world where children are taken and women are destroyed from the inside out; it is a world where men strap bombs to their chests in the name of god and where wars rage in the name of power. We are knocked by storms and famine and whole generations wiped out by disease; we live in a world which cracks and crumbles and erupts without warning. This world is more than grey at times, sometimes it is as black as tar, as evil as we can imagine.

This darkness can numb us and seem to overpower us and easily convince us that the task before us is too great or too dangerous. Fear screams into our heads that we don't know the path ahead, that it may all be in vain, that we may just make it worse if we upset the apple cart. But have you ever noticed that a nightmare always seems greater in the darkness of the night? When the light streams in the next morning, we can see the nightmare for what it is - light gives us perspective. Jesus Christ is the light that brings perspective to our world. He did that when He walked on it 2000 years ago and He highlighted it most strongly when He died and rose again. The darkness is there, for sure, but it cannot get around the light; the light that shines in the darkness which simply cannot understand it. Jesus brings us dawn; He flings His light into the evil around us and shows it up for what it is.

Much of the extraordinariness that we are called to is to act like tiny prisms that catch the light and reflect it out into the world around us. We are not the light, but our actions can show Jesus' light to those who need their darkness to be broken. We need to ask God to break our fear of the darkness in order to be part of the solution to the brokenness we see around us. There is so much hurt and injustice in our world and God is a God of justice. He vehemently reacts against injustice and He wants us to do the same by using all we can to bring Him to every dark corner.

He needs your snowflake. He needs your uniquely crafted, individual, different from any other ever made snowflake. You may feel that you are just too small, too insignificant, and too unimportant - but have you seen the effect of an avalanche? Don't tell me that snowflakes can't make a difference. You see, we were never meant to do this alone; we have been placed in communities and networks to join our little snowflake with others around us.

I don't know what your 'thing' is, I don't know what you love to do, what drives you on, what sparks fire in your belly; I do know that you won't be alone in it. There are others out there, others who want to fight for what you do, who love to do what you do and can spur you on, people with similar passions and similar gifts. There are your friends and your communities who may look different from you but, when you're joined with them, become a force to be reckoned with. They need your snowflake. Think of the amazing charities that make incredible changes round the world - they probably started with one person with a passion to see change, encouraged by another, supported by another, and joined by more and more who got on the same band wagon. You are not called to change the world on your own; you're called to add your bit to the millions who are doing their bit. Bring what only you can, offer what's in your hand; allow the fire in your belly to drive you to stand up and be counted for something you believe in.

You may just be the snowflake needed to help pour a covering of fresh clean grace on a situation which is grey and murky. Together we can do our part to reflect the light and banish the darkness back just a shade more. Maybe you are called to be part of an avalanche that roars with force and destroys obstacles in its path, that knocks down injustices with the talents you have been given, maybe God is on the move and He needs you to be part of His tremendous force for change.

The darkness would lie to you and say that you are insignificant but darkness in not actually a 'thing'. Darkness is the absence of something - the absence of light. The darkness cannot control you; all you need to break it is turn the light on it. It's a lie that you are unimportant or insignificant; it is a lie that hopes to scare you into inaction and fear because the darkness knows that it can have as little impact on stopping the light as a tiny tree does in the wake of an avalanche.

You are unique, every snowflake is. Every single beautiful one - crafted and created especially. You have been made to bring grace to situations, to join with others in causing a movement of epic proportions and more than anything else, to reflect the hope-giving, heart-healing, sin-washing light of our Saviour to a world which is crying out for someone to show them the answer.

Pause and Ponder: Snowflakes

'We can look at our snowflake... and ask ourselves what difference we can make'.

Do you believe that your life can make a difference?

'Much of the extraordinariness that we are called to is to act like tiny prisms that catch the light and reflect it out into the world around us.'

How can you reflect Jesus' light to those in darkness around you?

'It's a lie that you are unimportant or insignificant; it is a lie that hopes to scare you into inaction and fear because the darkness knows that it can have as little impact on stopping the light as a tiny tree does in the wake of an avalanche.'

Have you been held back by fear of inadequacy or fear of the darkness?

Who, Me?

I remember a friend once asking me the question - if you could do anything and you knew you could not fail what would you do? It's often a tough question to answer, but my aim with this book was to ask you this question in a roundabout sort of way. If at any point during the reading of the words in the book or in the pondering of your life or yourself, you have dared to believe that you are in fact extraordinary, then you are on the way to answering this question.

The first step is to believe it possible to live a life that matters and has purpose. So often we end up ruling ourselves out because we can barely believe that someone like 'me' can do something inspiring. You can live an extraordinary life.

Who, me?
Yes, you.
I don't need to know you personally to say that because nothing can ever take away from you, that you were built with eternity in mind.

In my exploration of living an extraordinary life every idea stems from this; every thought is laced with it. If we were simple accidents, born to die, there would be no need for us to make a difference. If in fact someone created us deliberately, then we were specifically designed for purpose. God is at the centre of who you are and who you can be, He has given to you and graced you and called you for His purposes. His arms are open to hold you for ever and to love you whatever. His heart is that you know Him and know how much He loves you; His desire is that you are found in Him and live in Him. He made you for a life of abundance, full up and flowing over, and He created you with pleasures and desires and hopes and dreams.

I have been convinced that I was laced with God's extraordinariness when He knit me together in my mother's womb; I received His DNA as well as hers. I am wonderfully His and He has planted wonderful dreams in my heart.

And so I am faced with a choice.

This choice is to believe God's promises and assurances or back down into the fear. I can choose to step up and risk my reputation, to stand out and invite potential ridicule, to believe even when others don't, or I can leave my dreams in a box, locked safely away from risk.

God loves me either way - what a comfort, what a promise; but I have been given one life to live the best way I can. I have been given tools and talents and experiences, I have been granted the opportunity to ask and be given to, to seek and to find, to knock and find doors opened to me. I have been blessed with God's presence and covered by His forgiveness and grace.

What more could I ever need to know than the fact that if God is for me, no-one can be against me? What greater promises could I have been handed than the one's already bestowed upon me?

On my journey to find my path on God's road map, I have found His favour and His grace guiding my way. I have been inspired by those who have done this before me and whose lessons can save me from pot holes and traps along the road.

I hope you find this an encouragement that you, too, are His, crafted and created for purpose, designed and designated to be someone who matters and makes a difference.

Your life is full of value, it is full of promise. Whatever dreams lie locked inside your box, I pray that you would risk them, take them out and share them, use them and believe that they can make an impact; not for my sake of course, but for the glory of the One who planted your dreams there in the first place; for the glory of the One who gave it all for you and for me that we could live a life in all its fullness; for the one who made you to be extraordinary.